Praise for *A Purpose-Driven Life* by Diane Pauly

As an avid reader, I love all genres; this book fit into so many: spiritual, narrative, adventure, memoir, self-help. Diane shows us how life's twists and turns and surprises shape our destiny. To read this story is like stepping into the shoes of an evolving guru!
—Peg Hau

While reading Diane Pauly's book, A Purpose-Driven Life of Helping Others: From Joy to Anguish and Back – A Memoir, *I found myself wondering how the bright, successful woman I came to know in her middle years had found her way through the experiences that have left others in similar situations persistently depressed and non-functional. And then I glanced again at the cover. The subtitle, 'from joy to anguish and back' and I understood that her tenacity and strength of spirit had traveled with her through it all; her inner guidance had shown her that a better life was hers if she could only find the courage to keep moving forward.*

I read Diane's book without stopping. I found her story compelling, interesting, well-written and engaging. She did not embellish the distressing moments which, for me, indicated a healed woman. She did not overly celebrate the successes. Again, for me, that indicated that Diane has emerged well balanced and wise.

Congratulations, Diane, on writing your life story that is sure to be on therapists' bookshelves and in the hands of those still struggling to get to 'joy.' You showed us it is possible.
—Marianne Helm, Director, Wholistic Health Counseling Services, LLC, Retired

Diane writes passionately and purposefully of her relatable life experiences, from pain to intense joy! A Purpose-Driven Life of Helping Others: From Joy to Anguish and Back – A Memoir *is about her journey from victim to survivor to thriver. Pauly is a determined life-learner, reframing struggles into opportunities. She transforms her life through self-responsibility and self-empowerment, finding purpose in helping others on their journey to healing, peace and love beyond fear. This book can help inspire the reader to believe in our ability to create a life of wonder.*
—Pamela K. Hertel, MS, LCSW, LPC

In her very unique style of writing, I found Diane's story, quite fascinating as it captured her early childhood memories of struggles and disappointments that she endured to just survive so many painful lessons of loss in her life. Diane has a free spirit and survives many years of hardship and brokenness. Diane's determination to make something of herself took her through so very difficult relationships, as well as not finishing high school and marrying very young to get out of the house because of the abuse in that household.

Diane was determined to make the best of life, and she did find the man of her dreams after many failed relationships. What rose out of the ashes was a strong spiritual essence, a love to be of service to those suffering and who were less fortunate. This diamond in the rough has shown her readers that everything is possible with God and that there is a plan for each of us, regardless of our present situations. Diane found that hard work, family, and her love for God and nature have brought her into the highest form of Grace, which is to Love and BE LOVE! Great Read!

—Rev Paul Funfsinn, Celebrating Life Ministries

A PURPOSE-DRIVEN LIFE
of Helping Others

From Joy to Anguish and Back
A Memoir

A PURPOSE-DRIVEN LIFE
of Helping Others

From Joy to Anguish and Back
A Memoir

Diane Wallner Pauly
with Judith Gwinn Adrian

Henschel
HAUS
publishing, inc.
Milwaukee, Wisconsin

Published by HenschelHAUS Publishing, Inc.
Milwaukee, Wisconsin
www.henschelHAUSbooks.com

ISBN: 978159598-926-0
E-ISBN: 978159598-927-7
LCCN: 2022944729

Cover photograph and design: Amber DeAmico

*I dedicate this book to my four beautiful daughters,
Pam, Wendy, Dawn, and Becky,
whom I love dearly and deeply.*

*You were at my side, every step of the way,
through thick and thin. You have become women
anyone would be proud to call their own.
I love you.*

From L to R: Becky, the author, Wendy, Pam, and Dawn

The Cold Within

By James Patrick Kinney

Six humans trapped by happenstance
In black and bitter cold.
Each one possessed a stick of wood,
Or so the story's told.

Their dying fire in need of logs,
The first man held his back;
For on the faces around the fire
He noticed one was black.

The next man, looking cross the way,
Saw one not of his church,
And couldn't bring himself to give
The fire his stick of birch.

The third one sat in tattered clothes.
He gave his coat a hitch.
Why should his log be put to use
To warm the idle rich!

The rich man just sat back and thought
Of the wealth he had in store;
And how to keep what he had earned
From the lazy, shiftless poor.

The black man's face bespoke revenge,
As the fire passed from sight;
For all he saw in his stick of wood
Was a chance to spite the white.

The last man of this forlorn group
Did naught except for gain,
Giving only to those who gave
Was how he played the game.

Their logs held tight in death's still hands
Was proof of human sin.
They didn't die from the cold without;
They died from the cold within.

Excerpted from 1972: The Answer is Much More Love, compiled by Fr. Gene Jakubek, S.J. (1972)

The end of all our exploring will be to arrive where we started and know that place for the first time.
—T.S. Elliott

There is no greater agony than bearing an untold story inside of you.
—Maya Angelou

TABLE OF CONTENTS

FOREWORD

I have known Diane Pauly personally over many years and many situations. In all of these times and situations, I have seen evidence of several essential qualities in Diane. One is that she sees reality very clearly, in all of its beauty and difficulty. This is especially true on a personal level, as she views her own life and the people around her. However, she has also had a personal experience of a spiritual connection with essential love that allows her to see the difficult realities of her own life and the lives she encounters with compassion rather than judgement.

In addition, she understands her own life and the lives of others in terms of possibility and transcendence rather than victimhood. She sees the reality of trauma and suffering, but has found enough healing and growth in her own life and the larger life we all share to allow her clarity and compassion, but also healing and growth.

This has led Diane to a deep need to share her own healing and the love she has experienced through a life of sharing and working to heal others. For most of her life, this work has been a direct sharing, using techniques she has learned through her own healing and others that she has learned over the course of her therapeutic experience. She has shared with women who have experienced trauma, but also understands how the trauma we all share impacts the suffering we inflict on others. This has led her to expand her work to include abusers to help them to heal and accept their own trauma, rather than inflict it on others in a vicious cycle. There are other forms of service she has offered that you will read about in this book.

Now Diane has felt called to share her own history of trauma, as well as her journey of healing. Diane would be the first to say that she is not holding herself as the model for everyone in recovery, and would share my knowledge that this is not offered for you as a blueprint, but as a story of how you can learn and grow from your own particular journey of healing. It is always an individual journey, but we can learn much from the shared experience and support of others.

One of the strengths of this book is that Diane has distilled some helpful experiences into particular steps that can be applied by others. They are laid out at the end of her accounts of her own experiences, in concrete suggestions for action and understanding. These are suggested action steps she has gleaned from these experiences that she can now share with others.

—Dr. Harvey Honig, Ph.D.
author of *A People's Guide to An Interfaith*
Christian Theology in a Time of Transformation

PREFACE

I never actually planned on writing a book but, as life was getting too difficult to bear, I went looking for answers.

First came counseling, finishing high school, and then on to college, which, at the age of 35, I thought I'd never be smart enough to do. Being older, I was more dedicated and totally enjoyed being educated about things I would not have known otherwise. It just felt so good learning and using my mind in a positive way, which was helping me leave my ugly, negative past behind. I still had a ways to go but was building confidence.

Next came many self-growth programs, joining clubs, and meeting new people, where we would sometimes share life experiences. I often heard, "Diane, you should write a book."

I never felt I had a story to share; I couldn't see it because I was the one living it. I tried writing and I'd get a couple of sentences out but it never went anywhere. I wasn't ready. I had more life to live first. Little did I know.

Then it happened. We had a substitute minister who shared her story based on the book she had written. At the end of the service, I spoke to her and asked how she got it published. She gave me a name and phone number. Bingo! I was ready.

I now recognized I had a history that could fill a book on ways to grow forward, on ways to see life through new eyes, and on gaining self-trust. I named it, *A Purpose-Driven Life of Helping Others: From Joy to Anguish and Back – A Memoir.*

May it help you find your way.

INTRODUCTION

For me, my life's journey has been to return to that joyful young child I was who skipped through fields of sun-lit daisies with my hair floating in the breeze. I don't know how real this memory is, but it is the image I want to hold. The attitude. In the intervening years, my life has ranged from breathtaking to heartbreaking and back.

But know that I choose to land sunny side up. I ultimately spun my experiences and life lessons into a course on happiness —*Happiness Comes from Within*—a sign that my journey continues to progress well. Here is my story.

I looked in the mirror. Blood!

It's 1956; I'm 15 years old. It was wintery and quiet as I stepped off the school bus. We lived in an old eight-foot-wide in Sommers' Trailer Court located in a wooded area filled with trees, bushes, and underbrush. The woods were barren except for the few stubborn rust-colored leaves hanging on for dear life.

My parents worked second shift so generally I only saw them on weekends.

Living so far out of town meant I had no access to bus service. My friends did not drive, nor did I, so I was mostly alone.

My list of chores awaited me each weekday afternoon. Wash the dishes. Put away laundry. Clean the bathroom. The usual. This particular day I felt the darkness and winter's icy claws. I decided to nap, but then the sound of slamming car doors woke me.

They hadn't gone to work!

Fear kicked in as I hesitantly greeted them. I could see it in their faces and hear it in the slur of their words. I could smell the alcohol warm on their breaths—again.

I had planned on washing the dishes after my nap. Now I felt dread looking into my dad's drunken eyes.

"Why aren't the dishes washed?" he demanded, slapping me as he repeatedly and rhetorically questioned me. I just stood, waiting for more slaps. They came. I was his punching bag.

Do I hit back? Should I hit back? The church, my parents, and society had taught me to honor thy father and thy mother. Obey! Do as you are told. Don't talk back.

I stayed frozen. What do I do?

Mom tried to stop him but he turned on her, hitting, hitting.

Dad had changed after serving in World War II. Why had he enlisted just as the war was close to ending? Prior to the war, my memories of him are all fun-filled. He had a sparkle in his eyes then. Post-war, he fluctuated between being that wonderful and beloved guy to being a man who was not well liked. Drinking made the difference.

This time, Mom hit him back, each of them striking the other. I tried to help Mom—who had always given me freedom and never filled me with fear in the same way Dad did—but suddenly I was on the floor with Dad sitting on top of me, slapping and hitting, slapping and hitting me.

Now I was striking back, trying to protect myself.

I managed to get him off. Maybe Mom pulled him. I don't know.

Standing up, I saw myself in the mirror, shocked that my face was bloody. Fear overpowered me and I grabbed a thin summer jacket and shoes. I ran into the darkness.

INTRODUCTION

Which way to go? If I ran to the road, he could follow me. No. I had to get away; it was all happening so fast. Thick clouds kept any light from shining through the woods and that darkness felt safer. I was crying hysterically. In the woods, plant barbs cut through the thin jacket. I had no choice. Run as fast as I could.

Was Dad following me? Was Mom okay?

What happened next changed my life dramatically with its twists and turns taking me in directions no one could imagine.

On the other side of the woods, I headed toward town, holding a handkerchief from my jacket pocket over my face as I passed people. Six miles to my cousin LaVonne's house; that's where I'll go. I ran on through the darkness.

What was my plan once I was at my cousin's house? I was 15 years old and knew no life other than living with my parents; it was life as it had always been. I figured I would stay with my cousin for the night and go back to the trailer in the morning.

It did not go down the way I assumed it would. I never went back to live with my parents again.

My aunt and uncle called the police. For the next two months, living with my cousin, I met with social workers and spent too much time in the principal's office. As I try to remember, I do not know what I was thinking or feeling. I suspect it must have been horrible not knowing what

Innocent Diane about age 10

was coming next. Sometimes it's a good thing when memory shuts down. Angel intervention?

Eventually I went to court, where my parents were in the same room. I had to tell the judge what had happened.

I was placed in a foster home with a *nice Catholic family*. I was told, "You will like it there." I was so scared and swore I would lock myself in the bedroom and never come out.

Were they a nice Catholic family? Yes and no. Husband, wife, and three children. But, guess what. The wife kept a glass on the shelf in the kitchen for her vodka, or was it whiskey? I don't know what her drink of choice was, but do know it was mood-altering. Unlike my dad, however, she was more likable when she was drinking. Her sister was not and I recall her once painfully pulling my hair and saying nasty things about me. I was accused of something—maybe of being a teenager.

Did I report any of the abuse? No. I never told anyone. Remember, I had grown up with abuse.

One weekend when the wife went on a Catholic retreat, the foster husband came into my room. I was in bed. He sat down, talking to me, and slowly started moving his hand towards me, under the covers. Fear swept through me when I realized what he was doing. I recognized the strange undertones in his voice, the way he acted, and the way he was breathing. A male baby sitter, my father's friend, and my father, had taught me how to recognize the signs of what might be about to happen. Was I subconsciously thinking that this is what some, but not all, men do? Are women just expected to live with it? How would I have known? I was still a girl, only approaching adulthood.

I screamed, "Get out!" He did. This only happened once. Did I tell anyone? No. When you're living in a foster home, feeling alone, who do you turn to?

Something we did as a foster family was pray together. It felt so strange. I went to church each Sunday with my younger foster siblings. I enjoyed singing the church songs as we walked back home. The four-year-old was so sweet and fun to be with. I have those good memories tucked away in my heart.

This may sound odd, but I am grateful for having lived with the foster family. For the most part, I didn't live in fear. I wasn't beaten. We ate as a family. We watched TV together. And I was not alone during Christmas. Somehow, this family was one of the sparks helping me envision a better future.

* * *

I do not want to paint my early childhood as entirely negative. Many times, I simply enjoyed being, doing, and learning. I loved nature and the outdoors, lying on the grass on summer nights and watching the sparkle of the night stars. I cherished animals. I was happy-go-lucky much of the time. In later adulthood, after many intervening trials, I consciously embraced this early joy as my chosen path.

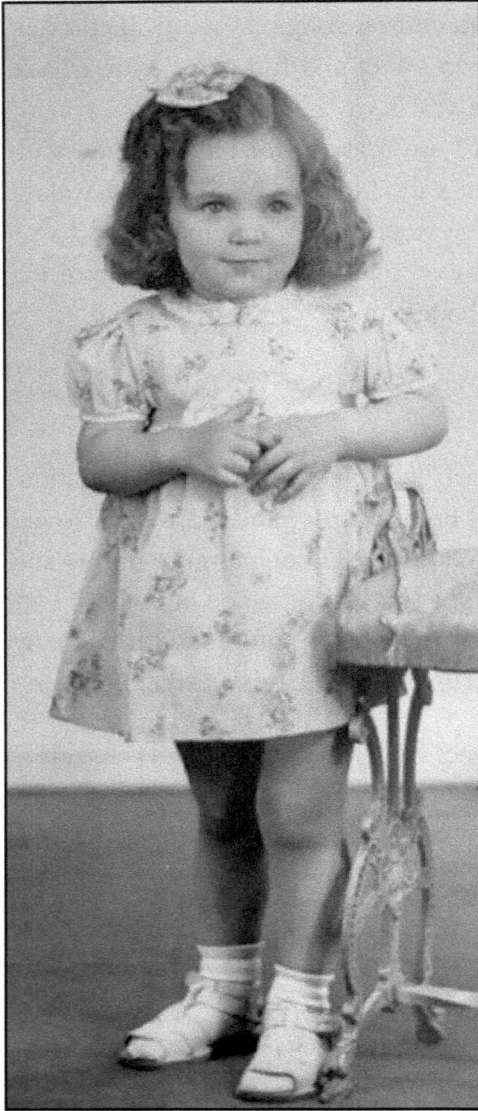

Diane at about age 3, in
Sheboygan Falls, Wisconsin

CHAPTER ONE
EARLY YEARS

I was unaware of the blizzard surging outside St. Nicholas Hospital on January 23rd, 1941. I was busy being born.

My dad, on the other hand, was following a wide-winged snowplow, trying to get to the hospital. He had stayed in Marengo, Illinois, working to support his family as we were about to add the fourth member. Me.

After my birth, we moved to Sheboygan Falls, closer to my mother's family. In the early 1940s, doors were not locked in the town and children played freely outside. My earliest memories are set near the Sheboygan River. It had a stimulating energy as water picked up speed approaching the cliff and ultimately cascading over the falls, churning and swirling. That thundering sound defines the town to this day and may have shaped my awareness of and love for the natural world.

As a boy, Dad had been raised by stern Austrian and Hungarian immigrant parents who were old school and believed their six children should be silent and obedient little beings. The belt was their preferred mode of punishment, which may have unconsciously surfaced in my father's mind when his drinking became routine.

While sober, he was an introverted, gentle, and loving man who felt other people's pain and was the father I knew in my early youth as we played and picnicked near those falls. A loving family.

Family portrait (Diane, Bob, Evelyn, and August Wallner)
about 1945

My father was present until I was three, returning two years later after his military service. I vaguely remember standing at my parents' feet and looking up as they said their good-byes. Mom was crying.

During those years when Dad was gone, Mom embraced the fun-loving, life-of-the-party person she was. Music, singing, and dancing were in her soul. Today, when I get goofy and let loose, I say, "Thank you, Mom."

With Dad gone, she took us to movies at the Falls Theatre on Pine Street and began taking us to the Catholic church. After our once-weekly bath, where Bob and I separately shared the water, Mom would dress Bob in a suit and tie. Prim and proper. For me? Cute dresses with patent leather shoes and a purse—my favorite was shaped like a little pink elephant. Mom was stylish with her suits, latest hats, and high heels.

The incense burned during High Mass was pungent and instantly takes me back to those childhood days when I smell it in churches now.

After begging her, Mom once allowed me to wear my new patent-leather shoes to school. After school, I rushed home through a recently plowed and muddy farmer's field. I was angry with myself for getting mud inside and outside my shoes. Mom's punishment?

"Sit on the porch and think about what you have done." Mom wasn't always gentle in her ways of punishing us. Sometimes we got a slap aside the head, using few words, but at the same time she gave my brother, Bob, and me freedom. Strangely, I was never afraid of her, that was just Mom being Mom.

My grandmother told me that during this time, Mom would lock the doors of our house while Bob and I were playing outside. Why? Perhaps she wanted time for herself to dance and sing along with the Big Band music she loved. Or, maybe she had a boyfriend. It is speculation. But I have no memory of encountering a locked door, but that doesn't mean it wasn't.

As elementary-school-aged kids, we freely walked the Sheboygan-and-Fond-du-Lac-Railroad trestle, looking down at the rushing river rapids. It was both frightening and exhilarating. *What if a train came? What if we slipped?* The childish sense of adventure outweighed any threat.

Not surprisingly, a town named after a waterfall is hilly. Imagine me as a seven-year-old roller-skating to school. We lived in the upper part of town, so roller skating down to school was doable.

Roller skating home was the greater challenge. I'd strap on my skates and walk in the grass, sideways, on the side of the uphill roadways. Why? Things seven-year-olds do are not always rational.

My fortitude was once challenged by a boy who reached into my grocery bag as I was leaving the store with items from Mom's list. He stole a cookie.

My first response? Shock. *How dare he!* Then, *What do I do? Do I dare take that cookie back? Will he let me? What would Mom say?* Did fear of disappointing Mom overpower fear of confrontation with the boy? Yes. In that moment, I gained some measure of the strength I would later need—and exhibit—in my first marriage, through the divorce, and in my formal education. The message that boy got was: *When Diane means business, back off.*

A part of the freedom of that era and living in the small town was that I got to be who I innately was. I loved those sweet ruffled dresses and, at the same time, I was pitcher on the 6th-grade boy's softball team. I loved climbing trees, twirling in the rain, and playing toy soldiers with Bob, although he always won the battles.

* * *

The impacts from World War II ultimately brought us hard times. For starters, after Dad returned home, Bob and I would be dropped off at church on Sunday mornings. No more fun times of Mom being there with us. Instead, our parents sat in the tavern until it was time to pick us up.

We often returned to a tavern with them, any time of the day or night. There was no such thing as calling a babysitter. One night, I fell asleep with my head on the bar, waiting to go home. Dad carried me to the car, scratching my beautiful patent leather shoes against the car door. I was not a happy little girl.

Sometimes, when we were in a tavern, Bob and I would dance like a little married couple. People loved it. We were usually dressed in our Sunday best. Sometimes we were given money. Other times, Bob and I got candy bars, ice cream, gum, and orange soda. Jack in the Box caramel corn was a favorite of mine with fun toy items like rings, whistles, figurines, stickers, and make-believe tattoos in the boxes. I saved those toys and collected them in canisters.

As Dad unraveled, post-war, Mom became the stronger parent, never complaining. Inadvertently, she was teaching me how women needed to step up and take care of family. She worked when Dad couldn't. Dad—who had never attended high school and had gone to work helping to support a family of seven when his father died during the Depression—worked random temporary jobs. At one point, my parents filed for divorce, but stayed together. When I asked why, Mom replied, "That's your daddy."

Reflection

- I believe very few people, if any, get out of bed in the morning thinking what can they do to cause harm to their child, or anyone else. Do you agree?

- I believe that humans, be they parents or not, primarily learn about life as they live it. It's like not really knowing what fire feels like until you stick your finger in and experience it.

- As children grow, words spoken in front of them, or to them, create confidence or lack thereof. Statements like, "You are bad," "You are stupid," "You can't do anything right," cut deep into one's soul. Phrases like, "You are smart" or "You are loved," feel so right and will take a person far in life.

- Have you ever walked into a room after people have been arguing? There is a negative energy coming from the screaming or yelling that differs from a calm or soothing sense. I could feel this negative energy in my home as a child.

Diane and Bob in Sheboygan Falls. Diane was in first or second grade; Bob was about three years older

Diane about age ten (school photo)

CHAPTER 2

MOVE TO SHEBOYGAN

My parents sold the Sheboygan Falls house and we moved into an eight-foot-wide trailer where Bob and I had to sleep on the davenport that converted into a bed. The trailer court was hidden behind Calumet Hall, a tavern and ballroom. I hated it. No friends. No open field to run and play in. Noisy adults often stumbled out of the tavern, waking me.

Too often, my parents were among them. I was scared.

One night after drinking, Dad decided to educate Bob and me about the birds and the bees. I was in second grade. Dad stood in front of us as Bob and I sat on the shabby davenport. He was talking and pointing to the areas between our legs. "Private areas," he said. My young, uneducated, innocent mind thought, *What is he talking about?*

As time went on, this *private area* thing was pounded into my head by a male babysitter—one of the few times we had a sitter—who lived a few rows down from our trailer. The sitter told Bob to sleep on the davenport and told me that I'd sleep in our parents' bed that night.

When he thought I was asleep, he proceeded to sexually touch me. I was so scared. *What do I do?* I stayed silent, hoping he would go away, which he finally did.

The next day, that same boy took Bob and me swimming. I loved being and playing in water. Maybe that's from the good days I used to climb on to my dad's back and we would dive underwater as I held on tightly. But this day, I was very quiet and withdrawn and that boy kept asking, "What's wrong, Diane? What's wrong?"

That's where my memory cuts off. I never told anyone what had happened that night, I was too scared and confused to tell.

Thankfully, we didn't stay living in that trailer court very long; the trailer was moved out in the country to 28th and Wilgus Road. Yes, I was glad we moved. There were tall corn stalks around us and the stars were brighter.

But now we also experienced animal smells when the wind was right. And some of them may have come because we had no sewage hookup in the trailer. There was a pee pot. Bob and I had to take turns dumping the contents in the outhouse daily. If we weren't careful, some of those contents spilled on our shoes.

I was still in second grade, walking to and from school now. (Okay, I admit I was that peculiar child walking with a cardboard box over her head on freezing days. It kept me warmer and yep, I did listen for cars.)

As part of an experiment at my previous school, my whole class repeated second grade. Although we were all part of the trial, it felt like a failure to me. Through the rest of my schooling, I was a year older than the other students and maybe that was what the experiment was about.

Bob was a scholastic wiz and overtly favored by our mother and her parents, as males often were over females.

I, on the other hand, was chastised for asking "such stupid questions."

Or for attempting to help Mom in the kitchen, to which she would say, "Get out of the kitchen, I can do these things faster myself." How could I learn? Dad once said that Mom should not have had any kids; she had no patience for us.

Mom was the one with the sharp words of criticism toward me, making me feel badly about myself emotionally. She had a way of making me feel small and like a nobody. I missed Dad.

Before the Kohler Company strike, while things were still going well with both of my parents working for the company, my dad and grandfather built us a small house with blonde wood throughout. It was cutting edge and stylish in its own way.

I got a room of my own. I now had my own bed and a dresser and vanity with a mirror and stool. I even had my own closet. We got a new, dark-green davenport, two casual chairs, end tables, a coffee table, and a wooden drop-leaf dining room table.

In the kitchen, there was a yellow-tone Formica table with chrome legs and matching chairs.

The doorbell played *bong, bong, bong* and I loved that ring. I was singing as we moved in.

Everything was new and fresh. Although short-lived, those were still the good days and memories for me.

On car trips, we would take a jug of water along. Dad watched Bob and me in the rear-view mirror and, as we took a drink of water, he would tap the brake just enough to make the water splash on our faces. We all laughed so hard.

Extended family gathered during those good days. There were card games. We set up tracks for my cousin's train set. We shared lots of food including Johnsonville brats that come from Sheboygan. Dad would lead us in singing his favorite song, "Peg O' My Heart, I Love You."

I finally made it out of second grade. Two boys were falling all over me, fighting over who could sit next to me on the playground. I had a crush on Ronald, but I was only a third grader, so don't tell anyone.

However, shortly after, both Mom and Dad began drinking more. Physical fights were happening. Bob would try to step in to stop them but would end up being hit as well. I stood back and watched. It was very scary.

As I aged—and matured, I suppose—Dad became stricter. He sometimes put me (or Bob) over his lap and spanked me. I found it embarrassing, painful, and it angered me that he would do such a thing.

Even worse was the punishment when he made me kneel on a one-inch by three-foot-long piece of wood, placed on a step. I would have to stay there until he told me I could get off. I don't recall how long that was anymore. But I know the wood left deep grooves in my knees. I didn't think I deserved punishments. I tried very hard not to cry—to be strong.

About this same time, one of my dad's friends sexually assaulted me as we passed each other in the hallway. I was on my way to the kitchen to join my parents and another visitor. His hand, so quickly, before I knew what was happening, went to that private area Dad had warned me about. As I pushed him away, he said, "You'll get used to it." I was shocked and scared. What was this man doing? What would Dad say? Would he blame me? Again, I never told anyone, but remembered this moment (and others) later, when my foster father came into my bedroom and I was scared and confused. Violated.

* * *

In 1954, 2,800 of the 3,300 Kohler Company workers walked out. This fight to unionize lasted for the next ten years; the longest major strike in American history.

The strike damaged Sheboygan County. The strike devastated our family.

Strikers prepare for possible tear gas during the Kohler strike (May 24, 1954, photo from Sheboyganpress.com)

The 1954 strike was the second Kohler faced. The first, also about unionizing, had happened 20 years earlier. There was violence and two strikers were killed. 250 National guardsmen arrived to control the situation. Mom told me that she and Dad, as teenagers, crawled on their bellies near the plant to watch the happenings during the first strike. Major events at Kohler were integral to life in Sheboygan, Sheboygan Falls, and surrounding communities. Additional strikes followed in 1983 and 2015.

Dad was raised to believe boys don't cry, which may have left him with few emotional outlets. He had only sporadic work as a result of the strike. His war memories, possibly including a woman he had gotten to know, lingered with him. Tensions and abuses swirled through the family.

Alcohol increasingly intervened, Mom began swearing and became adept at telling dirty stories. She changed.

* * *

When I was in seventh grade, age 13, we sold the house and moved back into Sheboygan, where my parents operated a tavern which was not a good idea since they were both drinking heavily. We lived in a dark, dreary apartment above the tavern. I can still see the glaring light in the kitchen that gave the room a hard look and feel. (To this day, I prefer soft lighting in my home.)

Because of the move to the tavern, I had to change schools again, but luckily, I was able to go back to Jefferson School, the one I had gone to when we lived in the trailer court behind the tavern/dance hall, so I knew a few kids.

When not in school, I was alone most of the time, other than spending some evenings with the neighbor lady. There was no TV in our apartment so I went down to the bar to watch television. I met lots of customers. I learned how to hold a beer glass under the spigot perfectly to get the right amount of foam. Sometimes I served as the pin-setter for the miniature bowling alley in the bar.

And then there were the nights Dad would get me out of bed after he had been drinking, just to talk about things. I no longer remember what he was telling me, which is probably good.

One night Dad sexually abused me. I had to push him away in earnest; my young, innocent mind was filled with a strange fear. And again, I told no one. I was too scared and confused. After all, this was the dad who had warned me about such a thing being off limits!

It's important here to state that the only sex education I had in school was about the chicken and the egg. I kid you not. I was too young to understand what Dad tried telling my brother and me when I was in second grade. My mother never spoke of sex or even the menstrual period. I had to learn about it the same way that most kids did in that time era, by living it. (Are parents still not talking about these things today?)

I spent Christmases alone. I remember once getting a pretty sweater with tiny white pearls on it from Bob. The neighbor lady I mentioned earlier gave me a Christmas present the year we lived above the bar, but I got nothing from my parents. On Christmas Day, they were next door at another tavern—you guessed it, getting drunk.

This isolation I experienced was partly why the (still in my future) foster family-time became so important.

The strike at the Kohler Company continued during this time and there were fewer customers, so less money coming in to the bar.

Somehow, I always kept a good attitude and faced life as it came to me. But I could feel I was slowly changing from that fun-loving little girl to a lost soul living in fear. I became afraid of doing anything to upset my parents, especially my dad. Fortunately, I still had lots of friends, but never asked them over to the house, not knowing if my parents would be drunk.

Time progressed and so did we. We left the tavern behind and moved to an upstairs apartment not too far from school on North 12th Street. There was nothing fancy about the place. It was old and a little run-down and located in a somewhat poorer neighborhood. I was given a bedroom right off the living room. The door had a window, which meant no real privacy, but that didn't matter because I'd rarely had privacy before that.

Luckily school was walking distance from the apartment. I took pride in doing well and wanted my grades to be the best and tried never to miss a day of classes. Besides, I would hear it from my parents if I did anything else.

Although Mom and Dad seldom went to church, they sent me to Catechism classes to be confirmed. In the Catholic Church, confirmation is believed to complete initiation into the Christian community. It matures the soul for the work ahead. Some classes focused on sin and only years later did I begin to question what that meant. Who was God? What was God? Still, I always loved hearing about God or Jesus, and angel stories and pictures. I often felt religion in my inner depths. My escape perhaps.

Dad knew the Bible well because his mother had insisted her children read it daily. I would get excited and listen whenever Dad talked about biblical messages and stories. To me, the epistles all say the same thing: *Love. Forgive. Forgive Them, for They Know Not What They Do.*

The pain and joy of my life continued. The irony of biblical messages, compared with my reality, was emerging. At times, the girls at school came to me to talk about their problems. I always had empathy for them and wanted to help. Maybe my compassion came from the secret life I was living.

Maybe this same empathy is what ultimately led me to my teaching career, a long way in my future.

During this time in the North 12th Street apartment, Dad would have fits of rage while drinking. Demons lived in him. He did things like pulling the curtains down. He threw things, including furniture. Once, he pulled the phone line out of the wall as I was talking with a friend.

I was filled with fear, especially at the look on his face during these extreme mood swings. Would it be identified as bipolar disorder today? Maybe.

My brother had announced he was moving to Colorado after graduation from high school. My dad was so furious at the news that he took Bob's clothes and burned them just before Bob was to leave for Denver. What else happened during those final days when Bob was still at home, I don't recall. Maybe it's just as well.

One night, my first boyfriend, Bill, and I walked home after a movie. From the bottom of the apartment stairs, we heard yelling and the sound of things being thrown. My parents were in a heated physical fight, drunk again. What should I do? Bill and I pretended nothing happened and we never talked about that night. Not talking about issues in my life had become a pattern.

I continued to find escapes. Seeking some privacy, I'd read entire books, while submerged in the hot and soothing bathtub water, leaving my skin so wrinkled. One book was *The Black Stallion*. Stranded on a lush island, the wild coal-black stallion approaches. Can I make friends with the beast? When I was reading in the warm water, there was no fighting. No abuse.

* * *

But fate had a new plan for me. We moved away from North 12th Street back into another eight-foot-wide old trailer, in yet another dark trailer park. The Kohler Company strike was still on and my parents needed to find other work.

They both took second-shift jobs outside of Sheboygan. We barely saw one another during the week. Because of where we lived, I was not able to attend any school functions. Again, no social life. Sometimes there was little food to be had.

From that fun-loving little girl of years before, I had now changed into a shy, very low-self-esteem teenager. Life kept getting worse. It was the only life I knew and had to just accept it as it showed its face; I knew no other way.

* * *

It's 1956; I'm 15 years old. It was wintery and quiet as I stepped off the school bus. We lived in an old eight-foot-wide in Sommers' Trailer Court located in a wooded area filled with trees, bushes, and underbrush. The woods were barren except for the few stubborn rust-colored leaves hanging on for dear life.

As I wrote earlier, this was the turning point.

This was the moment when Dad beat me until the blood came.

This was when I ran to my cousin's house.

This was when my aunt and uncle, who had to have known about my parents' drunken fighting, called the police. They understood the very real danger I was in. I remember my cousin's shaken reaction when she saw my face, swollen and covered in blood.

I held back my tears as I told my cousin LaVonne about Dad beating me and my running through the woods and across town all the way to her house. I was so worried about Mom. Had he hurt her after I ran?

I had to be strong. I had to be tough, for me!

Reflections

- Parents, teachers, churches, institutions, environments, and experiences play a huge role in who we become, all helping to create learned behaviors which feed our subconscious, or, put another way, they program the human computer we call a brain.

- Most of us engage in battles with our subconscious mind as we try to undo any negative programming we received as children, not always recognizing the struggles because the programming is so deep.

- As I look back at my life with my parents, I can't blame them entirely for the people they were. As I think of how they were raised and experienced life, I can see how their minds were taught, by their life journey, to conform to many behaviors, and beliefs that did not always benefit them. Or me.

- What does your human computer brain tell you is real and critical to your life and survival? How has that impacted the direction your life journey has taken?

Phillip and Diane
(1966)

Diane's wedding dress—
actually her church dress that
she wore for the wedding on
July 14, 1958

CHAPTER 3
PHILLIP AND MARRIAGE

The court sent me to the foster home, which was generally a positive experience. I was finally able to go to Central High School, my dream, (after all, Bob had graduated from that school).

Then Phillip came into my life.

During the summer, street dances were held behind the school. Student bands played. Those parties were filled with excitement as we danced, laughed out loud, and just hung out with school buddies. (Besides going to Central High, an advantage of living in the foster home was that now I lived in the city and could attend school functions. Yay!)

That one memorable night, I heard a voice talking to me at the street dance. I looked at him. *Who was this John Travolta-looking guy?* Slim. Thick, dark hair, combed back.

We spent the rest of the evening talking. Boy-girl conversation. When the music and dancing ended, Phillip asked if he could take me home. I did not know what to say, feeling flattered and thrilled at the same time. Haltingly I said, "Yes."

Later, when people asked, "Where did you and Phillip meet?" The answer was always, "We met in the gutter," you know, curb-side. Maybe there was more to that mischievous response than I knew.

Phillip was 17 and had a car. As a teenager in those days, dating a boy with a car was big stuff. We dated for two years and he came to know my parents, and the family situation, quite well.

But what happened next was unexpected. My parents moved to Illinois for work, probably after having been fired from their jobs. What this meant for me, being underage, was that Wisconsin could no longer care for me in the foster system. After finishing my sophomore year at my beloved Central High, the state put me on a train to join my parents in Illinois. I had no family or friends I could run to in Illinois if I felt I needed to. Was it a time to be scared? You bet!

Phillip and I were so young, but in our defense, we did what we felt we had to do. Life has a way of steering us in directions we don't always plan or expect.

Did Phillip save me from having to stay in Chicago with my alcoholic parents? Did I owe him my life for having protected me?

We decided to ask my father if he would sign for me so we could get married. I was shaking in my boots getting up the courage to ask my dad that question. I didn't dare ask when he was drinking.

Dad's reply, "No, you're going to finish school and then get a job."

Phillip and I discussed trying to get pregnant. But there was not enough time for that. Then Phillip had another idea.

"Let's go to a Southern state to get married. I've heard that the marriage age there is 16 for girls."

"Really? If that's the case, lets' do it!" Our only question was, *How will we get away?*

It came to me. "Dad, would it be alright if I took the train to Sheboygan this coming weekend? I sure would like to see everyone. I'll be back on Monday."

I was scared silly knowing what Phillip and I were planning, hoping Dad wouldn't notice my nervousness.

"Okay you can go, but you be sure to be back here on Monday." I was surprised that he agreed, but took advantage of the moment.

PHILLIP AND MARRIAGE

I packed as much as I could without drawing suspicion, thinking all the while that I was never returning to Chicago, and my parents, again. When we got off the train in Sheboygan, Phillip gave me an engagement ring. It was official.

Phillip's parents knew what we were planning and we stayed at their home. They understood why. Before we could get married, we needed to get blood tests, which we did.

We drove to southern states, but learned the age limit had changed from 16 to 18. We stopped at courthouse after courthouse.

One judge asked, "Do your parents know you are getting married?"

"No, they don't."

I was raised never to lie, and I was not able to that day. Fear came up inside of me at the thought of lying. Would there be punishment, be it from parents or church/God?

The judge said, "Sorry, I can't help you. I married a young couple the other day and the girl wasn't 18 as the new law requires. I got in trouble."

I thought it was strange that he shared that.

We drove back to Sheboygan and Phillip's parents. Unmarried.

What next? I got official paper copies of my birth certificate (multiples in case I made a mistake) and changed my birthdate from 1941 to 1940. No one asked why I needed the copies. With careful typing, I lined up the numbers and bingo, I was 18 and old enough to get married.

We were rushing. My parents were calling asking, "Where is Diane? Why isn't she back here?" Phillip's mother was covering for us, actually lying for us.

"Diane and Phillip have gone up north to visit some relatives of ours."

What might my parents do if I did not get back to Chicago soon? The pressure was on.

We decided to get married in Menominee, Michigan, where the waiting period was three days, rather than the five days Wisconsin required for marriage.

It was the month of July 1958, and we were finally on our way to get our marriage license, with blood tests and birth certificates in hand.

We were feeling nervous and happy all at the same time. The sun was shining brightly that day, birds were singing, the country side looked natural with its farm lands of rolling hills, corn fields, and wild flowers in their gold, white, and blue hues. Everything seemed brighter since the stress of worrying about my parents would soon be over.

You may be wondering why there was such emphasis on legal marriage as the way out of the situation with my parents. The late 1950s was another time. Literally. Women had little power—we couldn't even make contracts or buy/sell property. Few of us had jobs and, when we did, we earned about half of what men received.

So, for me to have left my parents at age 17, a junior in high school, would have been a violation of societal norms as well as leaving me stranded. Marriage was the alternative. But, did we really have any idea of what we were doing with a forged birth certificate, lack of parental permission, and me only having completed two years of high school? I would never graduate from my beloved Central High.

We finally found the Menominee courthouse and handed the papers to the clerk who said, "I can't accept these blood tests; they aren't signed by the doctor."

"What do you mean!?"

She calmly said, "Look at this blank line marked *doctor's signature*."

"What do we do now?"

"I can't give you a marriage license without the signature on the blood tests. You will have to get them signed and come back."

We sped the two hours back to Sheboygan, hoping the doctor would be in his office. He was.

The tests were signed and we were off to Michigan again, trying to get there before the courthouse closed at 4pm. Phillip was exhausted from all the driving so I took over. I couldn't stop my feet and legs from shaking as I was going around 90 miles per hour, and even passed a sleepy policeman who either did not see me, or ignored us.

We got to the courthouse with four minutes to spare.

Three days later, we returned to Menominee, having no idea where we would get married. We stayed away from the Catholic church because we knew no priest would marry us.

Other than that, it did not matter what denomination the church was. We stopped at a minister's home and he welcomed us in. He had a kind face and a warm energy that made us feel accepted.

"What can I do for you?"

"We would like to get married. Would you be so kind as to perform the ceremony?"

"Do you have a marriage license?" he asked.

We handed him the paper and then stated, "We have no one to stand at our side to be witnesses. Can that stop us from getting married?"

"Not at all. I will be glad to do that. My wife and the neighbor lady can be the witnesses. If you come back at 6:00pm, I'll perform the ceremony then; how does that sound?"

"Wonderful! We will be back at 6:00 sharp!" We found a restaurant, had a hamburger, and wasted time until the final hour.

When we returned, we both said, "I do." And that was that. It all went so fast. We were married on July 14, 1958.

Do I remember the name of the church, the minister, or the denomination? No, I don't. What should getting married feel like? Was it romantic? At the time, it must have seemed so, but as I look back it's hard to think of it that way. Should we have selected our witnesses? Should I have worn something other than my going-to-church mint green dress? Wasn't I supposed to have flowers? Where are the pictures of the ceremony? Should family and friends have been there? I did not feel married. But at least we did have wedding rings.

That was 63 years ago and we were in a hurry to get married. We divorced 19 years later, but so much intervened during those years. This is just the beginning of the story.

Yes, Phillip did save me from living in Chicago with my alcoholic parents. That much was clear. But I was so not looking forward to telling my parents I was married. *What do I say? How do I say it? What will they say?*

I was filled with fear, fear of my dad and what he might do when he was drinking. I knew what he was capable of.

Mom answered the phone when I called and, after asking where I was, said, "Did you and Phillip get married?" Yet today, I can feel these words coming from me.

"Yes, we did."

It was done.

Years later I found out that my parents had later come to Sheboygan to consult an attorney about getting the marriage annulled. They were told to forget about it because I would be turning 18 in a few months, and of legal age.

* * *

We lived with Phillip's parents until we could find a place of our own. They were very nice to me and we got along well. I was surprised to see that Phillip's mom did things for her family that they could easily have done for themselves. Was a fork missing from the table? She'd get up and grab one. In our house, the kids got their own.

Ironically, the cheapest place we could find to rent was an old eight-foot-wide trailer in that same trailer park where I had lived with my parents before being sent to the foster home.

We went from relative to relative asking what they had in the way of dishes, kettles, towels, bed sheets, or anything they no longer needed. We had nothing. I remember starting with only one big kettle for cooking. We allowed ourselves to eat out once a week at Schulz's Lunch, which was owned by my mother's sister.

I soon learned that this friendly, charming, outgoing, hot-blooded young male always wanted his way with me, any time of the day, even if I said no. He would force himself on me to fulfill his desires. In time, this escalated into physical fights. After having fought off my drunken father over the years, I was very good at defending myself against Phillip. The physical fights dissipated over time; that was a good thing. As I look back at those times, I'm able to see how there was no respect for me as a person. That disrespect carried throughout our 19 years of marriage.

Within a few months of the Menominee wedding, we were married again in a Sheboygan Catholic church, with only a couple of family members but no friends. This was a quick wedding just as the first wedding was. We were married in the priest's office. It was like filling an obligation to the church.

But what I most remember is the mandatory Catholic pre-wedding counseling from the priest. The Church admonished me to, "Always do whatever your husband asks you to do." (Remember, this was back in 1958. That was only one of the ways women were totally brain-washed in those days.)

Today, I feel anger when I think of those words and their meaning. Those words were not spoken to Phillip. I was so blind and obedient then because of the way I had been raised by my parents, teachings of the church, and society in general. *Honor your father and mother, never talk back, and do as your husband wishes, even if you don't want to.*

I ultimately learned that no one is any better than I am and I'm no better than they are. I'm free now to live my own life and make my own decisions. It took extensive work to learn this, but I made it.

Next came Phillip's and my grandparents asking, "How come you're not pregnant yet? It's been six months since you got married. Is something wrong?"

No, there was nothing wrong.

To bring in some money, I took a job at Wigwam Mills, Inc. working with yarn for making socks. Before long, though, I was pregnant with my first baby. I was strong and healthy throughout, as I was with my three subsequent pregnancies.

In due course, we had four daughters.

On October 25, 1959, Phillip and I waited together in the Sheboygan Memorial Hospital labor room. I was in intense pain for hours before my little girl, Pamela, was born. Fathers were not allowed in the delivery room then and it was standard medical practice to administer anesthesia to the mother just before the final stages of giving birth. In other words, I was put to sleep an instant before my baby girl entered this world.

It wasn't until I gave birth to my third daughter that I learned what I had missed having been put to sleep at the last stage.

Mothers and babies routinely stayed in the hospital for four or five days at that time. I loved looking into my little Pammy's eyes and at her sweet face. She had such tiny hands and feet, soft silk skin, and black hair like her father. She weighed just under seven pounds. The pain was soon forgotten as I held this precious baby. It felt so strange and beautiful all at the same time and I love the memories. Where once we were a family of two, now we were three. One of God's gifts.

We were given baby bottles before leaving the hospital. Enfamil and Similac were popular brands of commercial baby formulas. Breast-feeding had reached an all-time low, down to 25% of new moms. There were no disposable diapers. Cloth diapers were rinsed in the toilet, rung out by hand, and placed in the diaper pail, later to be washed and, in our case, hung out to dry because I could not afford to pay extra for the trailer park's dryer. Pammy and I both enjoyed bath time and, for me, that feel of a baby's silken skin.

Phillip was not helpful taking care of Pam: feeding, changing diapers, getting her dressed, putting her to bed, pushing her stroller, or even holding her.

Those were my jobs and most men I knew in those days didn't feel they needed to help. Taking care of the children was the wife's duty.

The trailer did not hold the heat well and I worried about my precious baby. One cold night, Pammy woke me with her crying. This was not normal. Being a concerned new mom, I had placed her bed next to the propane heater, located in the middle of the trailer. I'd piled on lots of blankets. Happily, she was just over-heated and I removed blankets and moved her away from the heater. A new mother learning to care for her baby.

Fifteen months later, our precious Wendy was born after three days of labor, although I will say that giving birth is something glorious a man will never know. January 26th, 1961. She had the same black hair and seeing such tiny feet and hands again warmed my heart. I was a little more educated on how to care for a newborn this time.

I was enjoying my life with the girls. I remember a warm sunny day when I was standing at the sink washing dishes with the windows open and singing a favorite song of mine, "Harbor Lights." I loved singing in opera tones—loud and clear. In the middle of my song, the downstairs neighbor called. He said, "I'd like to put in my request for "Far, Far, Away."

"Of course," I responded. He was having fun; we had a good laugh. He never said if I sounded good or not. And in church I especially liked the singing part and would sing out loudly and clearly in my favorite opera style. My girls, embarrassed at my display, would look at me like," Mom, do you have to?"

When we had a little more money coming in, we first purchased a trailer (to avoid rent payments), and then for the next four years, we moved to an apartment upstairs from my cousin, which was the same place I had run to before going to the foster home.

After we moved to the apartment, we had that trailer towed to Little Sturgeon Bay, Wisconsin, ironically to a space behind a tavern and close enough to water that we had access to a pier. Along with the two kids, we had added an easy-going German Shephard, Lucky, who loved the water. One of her tricks was to bury her head in the water and come up with a rock in her mouth that she would take to the shore and deposit on the bank.

One day, Phillip heard an unusual noise while we were sitting in the trailer. It was Lucky who had climbed in the bathtub and was blowing her nose into the drain. Each time she did that, she would tilt her head and listen. With each blow into the drain, that strange noise we were hearing came out of the trailer pipes.

After two years, we sold the trailer. I had learned that there was an expectation I would be the maid, keeping the trailer (and our apartment) clean while doing all of the cooking and taking care of the kids.

Women's lib was just being born and I had two daughters to raise.

PHILLIP AND MARRIAGE

Reflections

- *Why be polite and nice? Why trust people?* Good questions. Early on, I trusted and if someone said, "The sky is falling," I would turn to look and say, "Where?"

- At the same time, I was often afraid to say hello to strangers. Did these kinds of responses come from the strict parenting I received? The abuse?

- I'm thinking about my father's family where the kids had to sit quietly when they had any visitors. Sit. Be quiet. Respect your elders. This was passed on to my generation.

- A part of me continued to be the happy-go-lucky human who loved the natural world. But then another part of me had learned that people can't always be trusted. What is your experience around trust?

Don't Be Discouraged

When things go wrong, as they sometimes will,
When the road you're trudging seems all uphill,
When the funds are low and the debt is high,
And you want to smile, but you have to sigh,
When care is pressing you down a bit,
Rest if you must, but don't you quit.

Life is queer with its twists and turns,
As every one of us sometimes learns,
And many a failure turns about
When we might have won had we just stuck it out.
Don't give up, though the pace seems slow.
You might succeed with just another blow.

Success is failure turned inside out,
The silver tint of clouds of doubt;
You can never tell how close you are,
It may be near when it seems so far.
So stick to the fight when you're hardest hit.
It's when things seem worst that you mustn't quit.

From Gene Jakubek, S.J., *The Answer is Much More Love*

CHAPTER 4

A House and Daughters Number Three, then Four

The red brick house we bought was in Sunny Side, not far from that trailer court I had lived in with Phillip and earlier with my parents. Among other things, I loved the ironing board in the wall that pulled out and then went back when no longer needed, hidden behind a small discreet door. Remember that these were still the days when clothes were ironed regularly. So handy.

We had a single car garage and nice size yard for the children. New home, middle class, here we come.

I dressed the girls in cute matching outfits. They looked like twins. Weekly grocery shopping was an adventure and the girls always got to choose one book from the child's book rack. After putting groceries away, little Pam would sit on one side of me and little Wendy on the other. I still have that wonderful feeling of us snuggled tightly together as we read a story and discussed the colorful pictures.

Phillip did not have these memories. As was customary in the 1960s, he was working while I was doing domestic undertakings and raising our children.

* * *

Our third daughter, sweet little Dawn, was born on October 7th, 1965. She had thick black hair, like her sisters. Another beautiful baby with the same special feel that only a newborn has. So sweet and so innocent. I loved it!

With Dawn's birth, the anesthesiologist was not available, which meant I was awake at the moment of her birth. I found out that the best part of giving birth—for me at any rate—was when that baby came into the world. I'm sure many women know what I'm talking about.

Giving birth is one of the wonders of the mysterious world we live in. There are no words to describe the beauty and awe of it all. My beautiful baby made her entrance into a woman's world.

With one car and three daughters, life was complicated. To pay the bills on things like our mortgage or life insurance, I went to the offices in person. We had little payment books that got stamped to show we had paid, and how much. No sending a check off in the mail. To use our single car when I needed it took advance planning. I had to get the girls up extra early in order to take Phillip to work. Then of course, I had to pick him up later too.

Surprisingly, my father bought me a car so I could visit them more often. I was not seeing them on a regular basis and we never talked about the foster home situation. They had moved back from Chicago because the Kohler Company strike had ended after ten years. The strikers who stayed out the entire time received a settlement.

Dad's drinking now kept him from working. He struggled daily trying to stay sober and actually lasted a full year at one point; I was hopeful about getting my fun dad back.

One sober day, he turned to me. "Be careful who you chum with. It starts with treating a friend to a drink at the bar, or maybe even a stranger you start a conversation with, who treats you back, and before you know it, the drinks don't stop flowing; they just keep coming. Over time it can develop into a habit." That was the only time that I can remember Dad ever sharing like that.

His sobriety didn't last.

First, Mom and I went to court to have Dad committed to the Sheboygan County Comprehensive Health Care Center, a rehabilitation facility that offered acute care for alcohol and drug abuse.

Later we had him committed to Memorial Medical Center in Sheboygan, which was known in the area as Ground Kohler.

The third time, we took him to Fond du Lac, Wisconsin. I don't recall the name of that facility.

Each time there was a legal process with many forms to fill out requiring our/my signatures. This was very difficult for me, after all this was my dad. I always hoped for the best. Dad knew he needed help, but he couldn't stop himself from drinking. He would be sober for a short time after coming home, and then off to the bars again.

During one of the times Dad was away, Mom had a stroke. She was 55. The damage to her left side improved over time except that her speech was sometimes slurred. One day when she called, it sounded like she had been drinking. I said something to her and she replied, "Diane, what's wrong with you?" I realized I was responding to the memory of my drunken Mom's words rather than a speech impairment from the stroke. I vaguely recall feeling—maybe anger—that she might be drunk. I had developed less respect for drinking parents and that came out, unknowingly, in my response.

Dad had lost his driver's license due to his drinking. One day he drove to a bar across town. Mom called me from her job at a nursing home and I told her I would go look for him. I drove from bar to bar until I spotted his car. There he sat on a bar stool with a drink in front of him and it was clear he was too drunk to be driving, even if he'd had a license.

"Just one more for the road," he kept saying. "Just one more." We finally left his car at the bar and I drove him home.

Dad was now encouraging me to get a job. "Get more money coming in." *How could I do this?* Pam was in school, but I still had Wendy and Dawn to consider.

My friend from the trailer court agreed to babysit. I was hired at the Kohler Company. A family tradition. This meant getting up at 5:00am and working from 6 to 2:30. I did piece work in the packing department, brass division.

One day, a group of tourists came through on a tour when a man came over by me and said, "Slow down, I can't see your hands." We were given a base rate and the harder and faster we moved, the more money we could make. It was move, move, move from the time I got there until the time I went home.

Now I was a full-time housewife, mother, and a full-time factory worker. Still, no help from the husband, although he wanted attention too.

Phillip had worked in the engineering departments of companies that manufactured small engines. He felt he was capable of repairing and selling two and four-cycle engine products and that he could run his own business. We set aside money for this. He and I contacted various lawnmower manufacturers to determine how much money we would need. What could be purchased on consignment and would the companies help us set up sales and repairs? How would purchasing and inventory work? We hired an accountant. The list of what was expected of us was long. We rented a building, later purchasing it, for the business on the southwest side of Sheboygan.

It required a lot of work to prepare for the opening. We painted, scrubbed, built shelving and workstations, plus setting up bins for inventory. In a small office, I would be doing the record keeping, filling out ledgers, writing checks, payroll, and anything else that didn't concern repairs. I learned about the products we would be handling or selling, and I was sometimes involved in selling lawnmowers and snow throwers.

I worked at Kohler all day and then went to our business. I was now working two full-time jobs, and being a full-time mother and housewife. I did what was expected of me.

It all kept Phillip and me busy as the business grew rapidly.

One day Phillip announced he was taking a motorcycle in trade for a lawnmower.

I said, "Okay, but then I want a horse for me and a pony for the girls." He got his motorcycle; the girls and I got our horses.

We purchased Brandy, a large black horse (like *The Black Stallion* I had read about while safely reading in the bathtub of my parents' apartment). Brandy was friendly but needed an experienced rider. I didn't even know how to put a saddle on a horse.

The girls also had a lot to learn about riding their good-natured pony, Skeeter. No way does a person just walk up to a horse, give it some loving, and then ride off into the sunset.

After boarding the horses for a while, I decided I wanted a place where we could keep them on our property so I could walk out to them anytime.

Shortly thereafter we sold our Sunny Side house and moved to the country into a 100-year-old small, square farm house.

It was on 20 acres of land, with a large red Wisconsin barn. The farm fulfilled my dream of having animals. In time we ended up with 14 horses, three dogs, and a number of cats. We also had gerbils and hamsters that were so sweet, soft, and easy to hold. I loved them.

With all these animals, the girls would go to the end of our 20-acre property, hide in a ditch, and make a Tarzan-like call. The animals came to the sound. First, a long line of horses, then a line of dogs, and finally a line of cats. What a scene.

Our lives seemed idyllic.

* * *

But then, one day, I noticed Phillip was acting strangely. I had gone on an errand. When I returned to work, he came out of the back room carrying what should have been a very heavy box filled with repair parts. He carried it like it was a feather and was moving quite fast.

He seemed nervous. I couldn't help picking up on it although I didn't say anything. I had work to get done.

I noticed his strange behavior again a few days later, as I returned from errands.

A woman worked with us now, part-time. She and I got along very well. We shared stories of things happening in our lives and laughed a lot.

But because of Phillip's strange behavior, my intuition started speaking to me. I didn't want to think the worst, but there was a nagging feeling inside me that something might be going on between the two of them whenever I was gone.

I kept telling myself that it was my imagination, but finally I couldn't avoid it anymore. I felt I needed proof; how would I get that? If I asked them directly, they would deny it.

I knew I had to do something so one day, when she was working, I told Phillip that I was going to a retail store, and would be gone for a little over an hour.

I left, feeling sick inside, knowing I would drive around a couple of blocks and head back. I kept thinking to myself, *Diane, this is foolish. This is your imagination!* But I was shaking in fear at what I might find out.

On my return, I was watching and listening closely as I approached the door. *Will the door make any noise?* No, it didn't. *I would probably find them in the office upstairs if they were together.*

I started up the stairs ever so slowly, listening, watching, and being so quiet. My heart was beating like a loud drum. Could they hear it? It seemed so loud but maybe that was because things were so quiet in the building. *Where were they? What were they doing? Could they hear my heart?*

I got to the top of the stairs and turned to the other side of the room, where I could see their shadows in the reflection on the open door. They were close together. Too close.

Just then Phillip poked his head around the corner of the doorway and saw me standing there. I could see their shadows clearly as they immediately pulled away from each other. I was shocked. My intuition had been correct.

I was filled with anger and confusion. *How could they do this? How could he do this?*

How does a person describe the pain when you feel it in the deepest corners of your soul?

Rage came out in the first words I spoke to them. Then, as I'd had to do my entire life, I calmed down and got control. Still, I fired her on the spot. But I couldn't fire Philip. He was my husband. We had three daughters and a business to run.

We talked it out. He promised nothing like that would ever happen again.

* * *

Things were going very well with the business and Phillip wanted to expand. We purchased a much larger red brick building and with the additional space, became a subsidiary for another business doing small compressor repairs, filling parts orders, packing items for shipping, and invoicing for the work done or parts being sent. We would be dealing with customers locally, as well as across the United States. This partnership worked very well for everyone.

We would also be responsible for everything needed to operate the business that included inventory and purchasing of parts as well.

We set up a franchise with the Montgomery Ward Catalog Agency. Computers were not in use at that time which meant the customers would come to us, place orders, and pick up and/or return their items.

There was lots of paperwork and we would literally hand-punch each order onto a piece of stiff cardboard-like paper, that held digital data for Montgomery Ward processing. The ordered items were mailed to us and then we called customers to let them know their order had arrived.

We now had five employees and as time went on, Pam and Wendy helped out as well. We had grown into a family business.

I was pregnant again and our adorable little Becky was born on November 20th, 1971. I got to hold my little girl in my arms while touching her soft baby skin, and looking at those tiny hands and feet, just as I had done with her older sisters. I was so blessed to have four beautiful daughters. The older girls fought over who got to hold Becky, feed her, or even change her diapers.

Reflections

- Why did I trust that there would not be another affair? Was I responding to what I wanted to happen? Is that how we often react?

- These are the kinds of memories that stick in our computer brains. All that stuff gets fed in there and we fight with it. We don't know where it came from and we have to sort it out. Perhaps that's the life journey.

CHAPTER 5

ANOTHER WOMAN ... WOMEN

Phillip announced he would be going to the weekly evening open swimming at the recreation department with his friend and that they would stop for a couple of drinks after. The recreation department also had swimming classes for children, so I went in to sign the girls up.

Innocently, I asked the clerk when the evening open swimming would be over and she replied, "Oh, that stopped a long time ago."

"Are you sure?" I replied.

So where had Phillip been going with his little duffel bag, towel, and swim suit for the past months?

I decided that I wouldn't say anything to him, but instead I asked his swimming friend how swimming had gone the next time they went.

"It was fun," he replied.

Later, when Phillip wasn't around, I checked his swim suit. Dry.

I let it go for another week and again the response was that the water was fine.

The next morning, I went in to work earlier than usual, thinking that maybe I'd catch him in something. He wouldn't be expecting me.

When I got there, things were too quiet. A lawn mower that a customer had dropped off should have been taken in already. It wasn't, and that was strange.

I opened the back door quietly and stood at the bottom of the stairs listening. I heard him talking to someone.

Who was he talking to? Why was he upstairs on the phone?

He should be downstairs working on the lawnmower repairs. It was just too strange. I heard him saying something about bath powder and things like that. There was a whole lot of sweet talking going on. It was no customer he was talking to.

I waited until he got off the phone before approaching him, again filled with anger and heartbroken pain.

"Who were you talking to?"

"A customer."

"You are lying. Who were you talking to?"

Again, and more urgently, he said, "A customer."

I told him I had been listening, but he still wouldn't tell me.

I then threatened to tell the wife of a friend of his about an affair that her husband was having. Phillip had told me about his friend's affair and he knew I was angry enough to follow through with the threat. Like the little boy who stole my cookie, way back in my childhood, Phillip now knew I meant business.

He then told me it was the new part-time person. Again? I was shocked because I thought she and I got along so well. Why would she consent to something like that?

Then I questioned him on the swimming lie.

"Where have you been going?"

"Swimming," he replied.

I told him the clerk said open swimming had stopped weeks earlier.

"She doesn't know what she's talking about."

"Then why was your swimming suit dry when you came home? I checked it."

Then came the confession. He had been going to that same woman's house that he had just been talking to on the phone. He confessed that at the beginning he had been going into the barn, after he got home, to get his suit wet, but even stopped that deceptive practice. Maybe he was too secure in the affair and didn't even bother to hide it from me any longer.

Now I was aware of two affairs. *Were there others?*

This was a marriage I had given my life to and gotten used to. I was being emotionally abused as a result. Did I feel I owed Phillip my life for marrying me and taking me away from my abusive parents and saving me from living with them in Chicago? And, now again, the teachings I had heard all my life telling me I was a sinner if I did not obey the rules of the church, my parents, and my husband.

I was slowly becoming a zombie, numb from life. I was not able to see myself as being equal to others. I saw myself as being less of a person than everyone else. It was like I was on the bottom pile of the human race and everyone else was far superior to me.

I didn't know how to stop the pain I was feeling. I felt so used. What could I have done differently? I had no one to turn to. My parents were part of the problem and had long been a sword in my side. My relatives probably thought things were fine since I was married, had a family, and a business. They hadn't helped when I was put in a foster home, so why would they help me now?

Divorce seemed out of the question. I hadn't even finished high school and did not think I could get a job without having that diploma. How would I earn a decent living? I had four daughters to take care of because Phillip had never taken fatherly responsibility where they were concerned.

Not knowing what to do, I stayed in the marriage. Once in a while, we would go out with some of his married friends, which we had done from the start. But they were always his friends. I had no friends.

One night, one of Phillip's friends turned to me and said, "Why don't you wake up and die right?" What did he mean? I can only imagine how horrible it must have been to spend time around me. My face must have told a story as to where my mind was. Zombie territory. I never said much when we were out, but Phillip seemed happy.

I continued working hard at our business, doing all the housework, paying household bills, and taking care of the animals. I gave up cutting the grass, which I had been doing as well.

Well, then it happened again. Another woman. Number three.

* * *

I had always found the need to stay strong, but this time the emotional pain sent me a signal. I needed to act. Something kept me going, but what was it? My guardian angel?

Only now was I finally starting to break away from those rules and expectations after years of abuse from the most important people in my life.

Then it came to me. An inner gentle voice said to call a priest. I was going to St. Peter Claver Catholic Church at the time. Father Dave answered the phone when I called. Until that time, I hadn't shared any of what had been happening during the nearly 19 years of my marriage.

I spent three hours talking to Father Dave. The words poured out of me and it felt so good being able to talk to someone who actually took the time to listen to me. Someone who seemed to care.

When I/we finally stopped talking, he turned to me, and in a very kind, gentle way said, "Diane, you need to see a professional. I can't help you." He gave me the name of a psychologist he knew quite well.

I went home thinking of what I had shared and how wonderful it felt to finally talk about my life with someone. After mulling about things for a few days, that inner voice spoke to me again and I knew it was time to call the psychologist.

He was another godsend and so kind and understanding. He asked that Phillip come in with me. Phillip went once, but had no interest in going back.

After I saw the psychologist a few more times, he suggested I go to counseling. He stated the help I needed would take a while and that counseling would be the better way to go.

Again, I took a few days to think about what he was suggesting and decided that counseling was my next step.

I started seeing Joan, a counselor, who did not tell me what to do or give me answers. She kept me talking, would ask a question at the appropriate moment, and then wait for an answer. She knew I had all the answers within me and that I just had to learn to believe in myself.

That was the key for me. Learn to believe in me.

One day when I was at my appointment with Joan, (we were meeting one day every week) she asked if I would be willing to meet with a group of women from that time forward. There would never be any more than ten of us allowed in the group and it would always be the same women.

I liked the idea right away.

It helped me to meet with women who had suffered, were confused about their lives, were feeling emotional pain, and were working at finding a better future. It took time, but I was learning that these other women weren't much different than I was.

The fears these women were sharing matched up with many of mine.

Going to counseling was one of the best things I could have done at a time when I was not liking me, or the person I had become. I went to counseling for over two years.

Whatever happened to that love-of-life, carefree person I had once been?

I wanted that Diane back.

I went to work.

Reflections

- Having a community makes a difference. Having a caring, thoughtful community with people who have had shared experiences can lead to transformation. Have you experienced this?

- I learned that I was as important as other people and deserved happiness, just as they did.

- I came to understand that change happens when the true pain exceeds the reward.

- I sought out that carefree little girl I had been and began the journey of finding her again; ending her zombie life.

CHAPTER 6

THE DIVORCE AND BEING A SINGLE WOMAN

Remember

What have I done to my child hidden deep within my soul?
Crying, reaching out to be heard—
Let me return to my connectedness with Life.

What have I done to my child hidden deep within my soul?
Asking, always asking—
And me not listening to its deepest desire of wanting,
Oh, so wanting me to Remember

What have I done to my child—
how did I forget her love of life?

—Diane Pauly

For more than two years, I went to that group counseling, re-learning to believe in me. Those years were very painful, yet releasing at the same time.

Fear had kept me at an obedient child stage for far too long. I was 35 years old, the mother of four, more like an adolescent (which is not easy in anyone's life), and still trying to find my way.

I had been so busy striving to please others that I'd forgotten I was once a person with feelings, desires, wants, and needs. I struggled with these questions. *Would people like me if I changed? Why did I feel so unlikeable?*

These questions, and so many more, needed to be answered. Counseling helped address the things I had kept to myself for so long, all the way back to when I lived with my parents. I had been so ashamed of them and how we lived. And then I had kept the trials of my life with Phillip to myself as well.

As women in the group shared their lives, I heard echoes of my story. I remember once saying, "I know exactly what you are talking about; I didn't know how to say no either." Simple things came out. Some women were afraid to go to restaurants by themselves; they needed someone by their side. Two women spoke of husbands who wouldn't allow them to drive outside the city. Many addressed the assumption that college was seen to be a waste of time and money for women. These were such simple things but very powerful. What I heard, and shared, was fear and more fear. These women were controlled by others: parents, husbands, men, women, churches, institutions, and traditions.

These women and I worked to deprogram the false behaviors we had been led to accept as truths.

* * *

Then, one day something awakened in my mind and I shook off the demons that had controlled me.

It was time to get divorced!

Filled with fear, I contacted an attorney I knew. We talked about so many things. I needed answers. Who would get the children? Who would get the home? The business? Would I be paid an alimony? Child support? How would Phillip be informed?

I made the decision that same day. It was time. I was scared but said, "Let's Do It!"

The divorce papers were served at our place of business. Phillip didn't seem too surprised. He might have surmised what could be coming; he knew I had been going to counseling, and why. He moved out of the house that night.

Phillip was very cooperative. My attorney and I decided how to divide the property and what alimony and child support the girls and I would receive. Phillip agreed to everything. He may have felt the seriousness of all that was happening, or maybe he was looking forward to it since he was already involved with a new woman—one who didn't work for us.

Phillip got the business. I got the home and all the responsibilities that went with it: the house, the land, the animals and, of course, our four beautiful daughters. I received alimony for one year and child support until the girls turned 18. He got to continue operating the business with the security it offered. A fair deal? In hindsight, it would not appear that way.

It was done. I was a free woman. No man or woman expected anything from me. It felt strange at first. Was this legitimate? Yes, it was.

I had a dream that night after the divorce was final and it felt so real! In the dream it was daytime. I saw myself coming down the steps leading to the front door which was open and a policeman stood there. As I tried to exit, he attempted to keep me in. We struggled but I was determined and pushed him out of my way. I saw a path and ran down it calling out, "I'm free, I'm free at last!" (Interesting how similar this dream was to the time I actually escaped from my father when he was hitting me and I ran away through the woods.)

But the exhilaration did not last. Within a few days, fear swept over me. *Did I do the right thing? What happens after alimony ends in one year? What about child support?* Pam would be 18 real soon and it wasn't too long before Wendy would turn 18 too. Dawn would be 18 in six years and Becky in 12.

All of this happened so fast. I had no friend or relative to turn to. No job. No high school diploma. I was 100 percent alone raising four daughters. I was truly a fish out of water. For three months, I sat, not knowing what to do. I lost lots of weight and wasn't able to eat even crumbs from a piece of toast. I couldn't sleep. I had never been able to cry. How could I, being dead inside? I had to be strong. No crying allowed.

I needed my counseling friends more than ever, women to share all this pain with. As I was in the waiting room before my next counseling session, I could feel myself wanting to cry. *Oh no, I couldn't do that. People would see me, what would they think? I couldn't be weak; I had to be strong.*

But when I got into the session that day, the dam crumbled and tears came pouring out. Those tears had been waiting for so many years. I was hyper ventilating. My fingers were stiff to the point where I couldn't bend them no matter how hard I tried. My face and mouth were rigid. There are no words to describe what that was like. I tried sharing my feelings with the group, but it was too difficult to get the words out. I was in such terrible mental and emotional pain.

Everyone in the room was quiet, sitting and watching a woman struggling to push out of her zombie personality. A rebirth of that little girl I had been. Joan, my counselor, was kind and patient. She let me feel the intensity, in that safe space, knowing that I had to go through the pain before I could grow forward. (Yes, Grow Forward!) She let me cry knowing that was exactly what I needed to do, to release years of excruciating pain.

Somehow, I managed to calm down long enough to get home. I had to be there for the girls after school. Having my girls helped keep my mind involved in what we were doing as the evening slowly crept on. I went to bed as soon as the girls did that night. Exhausted.

Being alone in the dark with only my thoughts drove me back to that place of intense fear and my tears returned, crying out to be heard: Release me, I've been in prison far too long.

I didn't know how to position myself in bed. I would curl up in a ball, then straighten my legs, curl up in a ball, then straighten my legs, again and again, crying harder and harder. Legs outstretched, then pulled up into a ball. I was not able to shut off the tears of distress; they just kept coming.

That night seemed to go on forever, wouldn't morning ever come?

Not eating, not sleeping, not being able to stop the crying, I knew I had to see my counselor the next day. I was so weak by morning that as I went downstairs, I had to hold tightly on the hand railing, for fear of falling. I managed to pull myself together to get the girls off to school and then called my counselor who, luckily, was in her office.

"I have to see you! I've been crying all night. I can't turn it off."

"Diane, have you been thinking about suicide?"

"No, I haven't, but I need help."

"Diane, can you come into the office?"

"Yes" was my reply. I felt so weak and drained that I didn't trust myself to drive and called someone to take me.

My counselor quickly took me to talk with a psychiatrist.

He too asked, "Diane, are you thinking of suicide?"

"No, I'm not."

After talking a bit more he prescribed pills to help calm me and hopefully help me sleep. I started taking them that night and they did the trick. I was soon eating and sleeping and the crying was under control. I did not stay on those pills very long—I did not want to become addicted.

After going through those hellish days, I made a firm decision that I would never, ever allow myself to get that low again. Never!

* * *

I needed to push forward and finish high school. The GED high school equivalent tests were the best alternative. After all, I was 35 years old and fearful. I had been out of school for what felt like an eternity. Could I do this? Was I smart enough to complete the self-study program and pass the tests?

As I started the program, my old computer brain began kicking in. I found out I was smarter than I gave myself credit for. Wow, I was doing okay! And motivation was high because going back to the hell I'd been living was not an option.

While studying for the GED, I met a man who knew some of my situation at home. He said, "Diane, I work for the State of Wisconsin Unemployment Office and think we might be able to help you through the CETA Program—Comprehensive Employment Training Act. Fill out an application. I think you might qualify"

What did that mean for me? CETA would pay my way through the GED program plus a two-year Associate's Degree, and cover the cost of books. My old anxieties kicked in and I was thinking, *I won't qualify.* The girls and I had enough food, a roof over our heads, and some money coming in although not a lot. My real fear was that our situation wasn't bad enough. But surprise. CETA accepted me and gave me the encouragement to keep going. *Face fears as you come to them!*

The GED exams were a breeze but now I questioned my capability to get an Associate's Degree. The classes would be harder. Was I smart enough? I remembered my mom saying to me, *Don't ask such stupid questions!* and *Why do you bring so many books home when your brother doesn't have to?"* These kinds of comments were planted deeply in my memory banks, causing me to pause before deciding to move forward. I had to think on this.

Counseling was helping and there was growth. Strange how it happened, but those former painful tears were changing to tears of joy. I attended classes about self-growth: Woman Within, Assertiveness Training, Positive Thinking, Life Career Training, Dale Carnegie Human Relations, and Public Speaking. I was absorbing like a sponge and awakening to a new way of life. My blindness was turning to sight.

* * *

Other than self-growth classes, I had not yet ventured out socially. After being married at age 17 and staying in that relationship for 19 years, I went from obedient daughter to obedient wife. What was single life like out there?

A couple of women from the counseling group invited me to join a bowling league with them. They were right. Get out of the house.

North Bowl was connected to Lamp Post, a disco dance club. Dancing hadn't been part of my life for years but I was looking forward to it. Almost immediately, after sitting down in the dance club, I felt a tap on my shoulder.

"Would you like to dance?" Feeling both flustered and flattered, I agreed. The first dance was a fast one, but when a slow song came on, he indicated he would like to continue dancing. He pulled me in so tightly that a hair wouldn't have fit between us. The song took forever. *Is this what men act like now? Is this what men expect when dancing with a woman they don't know and have never danced with before?*

Relieved when the song ended, I rejoined my friends, but got another shoulder tap and looked up to a different man. *Thank goodness. Let's give this man a try and hope for the best.*

He was very polite and a good dancer. When it was time to go home, I got my jacket and he was leaving then too. I said goodbye and left, but noticed head lights in my rear-view mirror. Something told me to keep an eye on them. I was still living on the farm and as I approached the city limits, that car was close behind me. I took an alternate route. The car did not follow, but then, at the next stop sign, it was back. The driver? My second dance partner. He had turned around and was behind me again. *Had he actually been following me?* Yes! I sped away, did not go home, and eventually lost him.

A few days later, I saw the same man grocery shopping with his wife and children.

What can I say? First, I was running from my father. Second, running from my husband. And then, running from a stranger.

* * *

Counseling taught me to face my fears if I expected to have a life. From the bowling group, I went to a Single's Club in Sheboygan where I was welcomed. Many of the members were divorced so we had that in common. The group got together during holidays and for summer picnics. It was positive and safe. Some of those people are still my friends today.

Then, with my four daughters, I joined Parents Without Partners. The group offered family activities, including a week-end camping trip the girls talked me into joining. "Mom, please! Nothing bad will happen!" They were excited. We borrowed camping gear and I, of course, was worried something would get broken or lost. I had no money for replacements or repairs. You guessed it. Saturday morning came with a chill in the air. Determined, we packed the car and joined our new-found friends at the lake. The sky got darker. The wind blew chairs and dead tree branches around. And, yes, the borrowed tent was torn. Not to be thwarted, we slept in the car. All of us. It was still fun.

Knowing I needed to continue pushing, hunting for that carefree person I used to be, I joined the Ski Hausen Ski Club. Being outdoors and playing in the snow had always been joyful to me even though I knew nothing about skiing. In the club, I imagined having fun with friends while also meeting more new people to add to my friend list. *Was I still fearing meeting new people? They might not like me? Was I good enough?* These thoughts surfaced, but, if I never ever wanted to get so low again, as I had that night after the divorce when I broke, I had to push forward.

Trying my hardest, I might well have earned the Ski-Clown-of-the Hills award, if one was given out. Slow down? I did not know how, so learned to fall over, and once into a mud puddle rather than snow, which was not a good look. It seemed that every mistake or fall I made was right in front of the ski club members. They were tolerant. Once, when a friend and I got to the top of the hill, we were commenting on the mattresses covering the posts supporting the chair lift. Well, me, not being any good at slowing down or making turns, I ended up smashing into the closest mattress when I got off the lift. My head must have looked like a Bobblehead figure bouncing off the mattress. My ear muffs went flying, my skis came off, and the chair lift had to be stopped as I was being helped up. The ski club members were watching.

Oh well, I was getting out and having fun.

* * *

The following summer, I frequented Bud and Lavern's Bar, known for socializing and dancing. In Sheboygan, women fast-danced together so I was able to do lots of the dancing I loved.

That particular evening, I was standing at the end of the bar when some bikers, dressed in black leather came in. One of the bikers came to the end of the bar to get drinks. He stood next to me and I noticed he had a colorful scarf, tied in a bow, attached to his belt loop. I don't know what triggered me to do it, but I reached over and pulled on one end of the scarf to undo the bow. Nothing was spoken between either of us. He took the drinks and went back to his friends across the room. *Wow! Whatever possessed me to do that!?*

Later, when he came over for more drinks, the scarf was retied. I reached over and untied it again. No words. When the bikers were leaving, he turned to me and wiggled his hips, showing he had tied the scarf back into its bow. It was like we were two little kids enjoying the fun thing we were doing. Double wow! Did I mention he was tall, dark, handsome, and easy on the eyes?

About a month later, back in Bud and Lavern's, he was there and this time asked me to join his group. Abruptly I was sitting and socializing with black leather bikers. Who would have thought? But then, remember when Phillip, my ex, took that motorcycle in trade? I rode with him and loved the feeling of being so close to nature. We drove to Florida and to the Indy 500 races once. But Phillip and I were not dressed in black leather.

As a result of my motorcycle experiences, Don and I got along right away, having something in common. He showed me his bike and we went for a ride that evening. For a short time, I became a motorcycle momma. Early on, he took me to a local biker's bar and introduced me saying, "This is Diane, be sure to treat her like a lady; show respect." I was not expecting that, especially with my history. (And, he gave me a black leather jacket to wear.)

On September 4th, 1977, we joined over 100 bikers riding from Sheboygan to Madison for a Helmet Rally at the Capitol.

Around 50,000 bikers attended this Concerned Motorcyclists of Wisconsin (CMW) event, hailed as the biggest rally at that time. The rally was about repealing a law that required cyclists to wear helmets. State Patrol and sheriff's departments did not interfere with the bikes who stopped traffic in intersections until all had crossed. Don and I had a turn at stopping traffic and we were among the bikers converging on the Capitol that Sunday. It was certainly better than sitting on the couch feeling sorry for myself.

Life works in mysterious ways and I was living. Growing. Experiencing what life had to offer. Facing fears. And all because I reached out and opened a bow.

Over time, Don and I saw less and less of each other, but I sensed he was a stepping stone for me. I had a lot of fun but I needed to move on. I didn't want to be a motorcycle momma the rest of my life.

What awaited me, in years to come, only time would tell, and tell it did!

Reflections

- My counseling friends and I worked to deprogram the artificial behaviors we had been led to accept as necessary realities.

- My questions? Why did I feel so unlikeable? Who was I? Could I transform myself? Would people like me if I changed?

- How did I get here? How could I have allowed this maid/slave life to take me over? I was learning to be strong, but was I expecting too much of me?

- What did I want? I didn't know, but was learning.

Today Upon a Bus

Today upon a bus,
I saw a lovely girl with golden hair.
I envied her—
She seemed so joyful.
And I wished I were as fair.
When suddenly she rose to leave,
She had one leg and wore a crutch,
And as she passed—a smile.
Oh, God forgive me when I whine.
I have two legs, the world is mine.

And then I stopped to buy some sweets.
The lad who sold them had duch charm;
I talked to him—he seemed so glad.
If I were late, "t'would do no harm."
And as I left, he said, "I thank you.
You've been so kind.
It's nice to talk with folks like you.
You see, I'm blind."
Oh, God forgive me when I whine.
I have two eyes, the world is mine.

An later, walking down the street,
I saw a child with eyes of blue.
He stood and watched the others play;
It seemed he knew not what to do.
I stopped a moment and then I said,
"Why don't you join the others, dear?"
He looked ahead without a word.
And then I knew—he couldn't hear.
Oh, God forgive me when I whine.
I have two ears, the world is mine.

With legs to take me where I would go,
With eyes to see the sunset's glow,
With ears to hear what I would know,
Oh, God forgive me when I whine.
I'm blessed indeed—the world is mine.

From Gene Jakubek, S.J., *The Answer is Much More Love*

CHAPTER 7
COLLEGE AND CONTINUING GROWTH
(1978-1980)

My growth was continuing, expanding into new worlds. Stepping beyond hesitations, attaining an Associate's Degree at Lakeshore Technical College, became my next goal.

The counselor suggested going into a man's field to earn more money after graduation. Materials Management was a perfect fit because of Phillip's and my business experiences. But remember that I had a history with men that wasn't all positive, so going into a man's field was a challenge. Still, I had to face the music and face it I did.

Materials Management classes would prepare me for manager positions in areas like: inventory, purchasing, transportation, packing, shipping, raw materials made into finished products, record keeping, business law, and how different types of machines were run; anything to do with factory type manufacturing. I would tour a couple of factories, see how their systems were run, and then write papers on the experiences. I was the only woman in the class and was about twenty years older than the other students. I soon found out the purchasing class professor favored the guys.

If an exam answer was marked wrong, he would allow the students to explain how they understood the question and then reconsider their answer. Usually he would say, "Well okay, you can have credit for that."

But when I raised my hand to explain how I understood a question, and why I answered as I did, his reply was, "No, Diane, I don't think your answer is correct. I cannot give you credit."

Then one of the guys explained his thoughts about his answer. The teacher listened, considered it, and started to say, "Well, okay, you..." At that instant, I snapped, pounded my fist on the desk, and loudly said, "Okay, you give him credit, but then I want credit for mine! By God, what's fair is fair!"

Everyone in the room looked at me. I was shocked. Where did that come from? Me?

I tell this story because *What's fair Is fair.* No one, but no one—male or female—is any better than I am and I'm no better than anyone else!

Did I get credit for my answer? I don't remember, but I do recall standing up for myself! For that short instant, I found my voice and was beginning to develop a line of intolerance. Cross it and watch out.

The teacher and I got along well after that episode and in another class with him, the Transportation Department, I finished first with an A on the final three-day exam. At graduation, he sent me a congratulations card. That teacher came to believe in me.

I too was continuing to learn to believe in myself. Feeling brave one day, I noticed a woman sitting in her car, listening to music and was thinking to myself, *What would happen if I tried talking to a total stranger? Would I dare? Did we have anything in common to talk about?*

I decided to experiment. In the lady's washroom, I saw the same woman combing her hair. As we stood there in silence, I was thinking, *What can I say? Will she ignore me?*

I feared possible rejection, which I had lived and experienced most of my life. *Come on, Diane, you can do it, you have to try.*

I offered, "I noticed the music you were listening to in your car as I was walking past and liked what I was hearing."

Not long after I started the conversation, we were talking as though we had known each other forever.

Another lesson learned. When I see someone with a frown or scowl, I ask myself, *Do I dare try talking with them?* When I do, nine times out of ten, they will smile, seemingly happy about the conversation. Sometimes there is even a hug of thanks. I think it's one of those innate things we are born with: the need to eat, sleep, keep warm, and connect. Humans just seem to need connection with other humans.

* * *

Two years later, I graduated from Lakeshore Technical College with honors and was handed an Honor Cord to wear at graduation. I was not expecting that and still feel emotional about it. I hadn't given it a thought when I was in school; just did my assignments, while also taking care of my four beautiful daughters, a home, and the responsibilities that go with it. My central focus was aimed at creating a new life for us all.

In some ways, this honor made up for not graduating with my high school class in 1960. Back then I actually had dreams for two years—which would have been my junior and senior years—of going back to school. Those dreams didn't subside until my class had graduated.

* * *

One day, I heard about an 18-week Dale Carnegie Human Relations and Public Speaking program, intended to build self-confidence. I was thinking, *Diane, this might be just what you need*, although the idea of mixing with people—especially men I didn't know—was unsettling. Still, it was something I had to do to continue moving forward and facing my fears.

Turned out, I was the only woman among about 15 men. We gave speeches on topics of our choice. Speaking became easier and I learned, by watching and listening, that the men were nervous and flustered too. I was getting to know men in a non-threatening way.

At one class, we were told that the person who gave the best speech would win a nice Dale Carnegie book. We could speak on any topic. There would be an imaginary line down the middle of the room and two of us, one on each side of the line, would be talking at the same time. *How on earth would that work?*

The first two speakers tried to out-talk each other by speaking loudly. As they were getting louder and louder, it became difficult to hear what they were saying. I surmised that getting loud would not do the trick. *How could I get everyone's attention?*

It came to me. A movie. A movie of one of my life experiences.

Sitting on a chair on my side of the line, I said, "I'm going to tell you about the time I gave my brother a bicycle ride."

Pretending I was pedaling, moving my legs 'round and 'round, I told them I had lost control as my brother and I turned a corner. Then I slid across the floor on my knees. It was unexpected. Sitting on the floor, I held my knee in a bent position, and in a make-believe, sobbing voice, said, 'It hurts so bad, it's bleeding. Where's my momma?' I told them my brother ran to the house to get Momma. At the doctor's office, they laid me on (sob, sob) a bed-type table. I was now lying flat on the floor while finishing my speech/story. They put something on the cut (sob, sob) and the dirt just boiled out (sob, sob).

I won the book that night and lots of pats on the back, along with a little more self-confidence.

Counseling, learning at the college and in Dale Carnegie, and meeting nice men in the clubs I joined were proving valuable. Not all men were like the ones I had known growing up and in early adulthood. These men had different energies, which signaled a comfort zone for me. And the more I faced my fears, the more fearless I was becoming.

* * *

Wanting to share my growth with someone, I went to visit Father Dave, the priest I had talked to before my divorce.

As I was driving, a mysterious godly feeling came over me. I was still seeing the road, conscious of my driving, but at the same time, seeing images that were speaking to me of love in this world, or lack thereof. The message was telling me that humans have before them every day, the meaning of life in what has been given them. All they need do is pay attention.

Love appeared in my vision as soft, cuddly puppies, gorgeous flowers in radiant colors, beautiful sunsets, and reflections of the sun glittering on bodies of water. It wasn't even the images so much as the absolute love feeling that came with them.

Lack of love came to me as images of the dark side of life: murky, ugly, broken, misshapen branches, and dead week-old carcasses being eaten by maggots. Along with the images came shadowy, heavy, horrible feelings.

There are no words to fully describe the experience that day. It was truly a mysterious, godly vision.

I was still filled with that awesome Love/Godly feeling when Father Dave and I began to talk. Telling him about the vision, the hypnotized zone continued, like I was reliving it and still feeling the messages and the images. Father Dave listened keenly to every word, and appeared to be feeling the intensity/truths of the message too.

When I finished his reply was, "Diane, I believe in everything you have said. I would add one thing. When you get to those Golden Gates, you will be asked, 'What do you choose?'"

It was all so real!

* * *

1979. All the horses had been sold and it was time to move from the country, and my past life, to the city.

Knowing the value of the house and land, I decided to sell it myself and keep the money I would have paid a realtor. Luckily, I knew a person who had already shown interest in the farm and he agreed to my price. We were on our way. Our two big dogs stayed on the farm. The girls and I loved them and it wasn't easy leaving them behind but living in a small house just did not seem like the right thing to do to them. The new owner was glad to have them stay and we did get to visit from time to time.

I then contacted a realtor to help with the next purchase. "I want a small house for me and my four daughters. It has to have maintenance-free siding and I don't want to have hammer and nail in hand when I move in. I also want a small yard—less grass to cut—and walking distance to grocery stores, filling stations etc., and a one-car garage." He called in a few weeks, "Diane, I think I found just what you are looking for."

The girls and I went to take a look at the cute little, light-yellow, story-and-a-half bungalow with large living room windows that let the warm sun shine in, giving a cozy feel. It had a small, well-manicured yard and a one-car garage. So practical. No house payments. The location was perfect and I could afford to add two bedrooms upstairs for Pam, Wendy, and Dawn, who got the smaller of the two rooms. Becky, being the youngest, got a room downstairs closest to mine.

What really sold us on the house? On the farm, we had one small medicine cabinet mirror, and I mean small. The new home had a large, and I mean large, mirror in the bathroom over the sink and counter. The girls and I were all able to stand in front of the mirror at the same time and still be able to see ourselves. With big smiles on our faces, we said, "Yes, this is the place!"

I felt so confident and sure in what I was doing selling the farmhouse and land on my own. I seemed to know what I had to do and followed through. I was so sure of myself. It was almost like I had a guiding hand showing me the way. Where was that strong inner guidance coming from? I didn't know for sure, but I was embracing it.

I need to include Buddy's story too. We brought two of the cats with us from the farm, but we missed having a dog. At the Humane Society, we found Buddy, a 12-pound, curly-haired dog. He seemed to like us so we took him home. He was quiet, sweet, and liked to cuddle. He only barked at the mailman who provoked him by pulling mail in and out of the slot at a quick pace knowing Buddy didn't like it. Naughty mailman.

Then Buddy started acting like he was a cat. I would find him walking on the kitchen counter. When the cats started spraying, he did too. It was sad, but we gave him to a friend and took the cats back to the farm. Later we found out that Buddy had been given to another friend who lived a half hour away.

With no animals, daughter Becky and I decided to walk through the Humane Society, not to get an animal, but to have the fun of looking at and touching those furry little creatures, those gifts of nature. Becky had gone ahead excited about all the wonderful cats and dogs she was seeing. All of a sudden, she came running to me, crying, "Mom! Buddy is here! Can we take him home?

"What? Buddy's not here. The dog you're seeing only looks like Buddy."

"No, Mom, it's Buddy. Please, can't we take him home?"

I figured I'd better take a look and it actually was Buddy. Couldn't believe my eyes. Our little Buddy.

He had been found in Sheboygan, a half hour from where we lived. Was he trying to find his way back to us? That could have been the only answer. We paid the fee and took him home, adopting him for the second time. With the cats gone, Buddy never marked or had an accident in the house again.

* * *

We lived in that house for twelve years and a lot had happened once I started counseling: divorce, GED, two-year Associate's Degree, singles club, Parents without Partners, Ski Hausen Ski Club, Dale Carnegie program, country home sold, and lots of new friends.

What I learned was that I was a strong and able woman. But then, what was this? One day, driving to my counseling appointment, old fear feelings arose. Where was that coming from? The following week the fear feelings had gotten stronger and I was sharing less with the group each week. *Was I going backwards? What was happening? How come I was not talking as much? What was I afraid of?*

Finally, when someone else was talking in the counseling group, I had to interrupt and share my fear feelings.

"Joan, I need to share what has been happening. Am I going backwards in my growth? Why am I feeling fear? Have you noticed I haven't had much to say of late?"

What followed was not expected, but then I knew Joan would always ask questions, helping me find my best answers.

Joan replied, "Diane, should this be your last time with us or would you like to come back next week yet?" *Blow me over, where did that come from? My last day or week? Wow, I wasn't ready to lose my support group.*

I walked out of there and crashed, seeming to almost hit rock bottom. How could I survive without my counseling friends? I always had someone to share happenings in life with. They were constantly willing to listen when I had to make decisions and they made good suggestions. Filled with fear at first, as the week went on, I began feeling better. There was my schooling. There were my new friends.

The following week, I decided to go back, but was ready to let go. I sat through the session and when it was time to leave, we all hugged and I sat there with tears of appreciation for those women. They have no idea how important they were to me. But on the other hand, I'm sure I played a significant part in their lives too.

I openly share the experiences of going to counseling when I needed it most. So many people helped me; I was blessed to have had such beautiful souls in my life.

What had happened in the group? I was all talked out. I had gotten all I needed from the support group. Now it was time for me to go out on my own. It's like my history was saying good-bye; it was time to let go of the past and create a new one. My counselor knew I was ready for next steps.

* * *

And then I met Tim, who taught me about jealousy and mistrust. We met through a friend and Tim seemed charming and polite. He was a teacher, which I thought was an honorable profession. We both liked movies. He played tennis and I was just learning, so before our first evening together ended, we had made a date to play tennis. Thus began our romance.

One morning, he called. "Turn your radio to WKTS." The song playing was "I Just Called to Say I Love You." He was romantic in special ways. We dated for a year and became engaged. He moved in with the girls and me and was so helpful around the house and yard; all those things that Phillip did not help with.

But change came slowly when Tim expressed that he didn't want me to do things with my friends, even during the day. If a man as much as looked at me, he claimed I was signaling a desire for attention from that man. If we walked through a crowd, he'd say things like, "Now's your chance to rub up against the guys." He also didn't want me spending too much time with my daughters. Jealousy was showing its ugly face and I had not lived with anything like this before. I was at a loss.

One evening when I did go out with a couple friends, he was irate. In anger, he went out too. I was in bed when he came in and said, "Well, did you have a good f***!" It was dark in the room, and in anger, when I heard those horrendous, unwarranted words, I swung out. He screamed saying; "You knocked out my eye." I hadn't, but by the way he screamed, I wondered if it was possible.

I needed to let go. He could be both so romantically nice and so unbelievably jealous. Was it mind games or plain cruelty? I go with cruelty. It hurt.

Then came the worst of his behavior when he exposed himself to one of my daughters. I immediately approached him but he already knew what to expect and moved out. Living through all that was another hardship and also another lesson to learn from.

Why was I such a slow learner in relationships? How had I been programed to be obedient to men? Was it my dad, who was loving and kind, but so strict and harsh in punishments when disobeyed? Was it the church teaching, Honor your father and mother? I had learned to live with it until the true pain exceeded the reward, which forced me to run away and get married at 17. And another church commandment. The priest looking me in my eyes saying, "Always do whatever your husband wants you to. If you don't obey those rules, you are a sinner."

Then there was the culture—the times I was living in. Television in the late 1950s often depicted men as heads of the household with women cooking and doing housework in dresses and high heels. (*Who does that?*)

From a 1950s home economics textbook that high school girls read in preparation for marriage, there were lessons like, "Prepare yourself. Take 15 minutes to rest so you will be refreshed when he arrives. Touch up your make-up, put a ribbon in your hair and be fresh looking. He has just been with a lot of work-weary people. Be a little gay and a little more interesting. His boring day may need a lift." And, "Listen to him: You may have a dozen things to tell him, but the moment of his arrival is not the time. Let him talk first."

Women were damaged by these contrived lessons, it is true. But men were as well. It would take the political women's liberation movement of the late 1960s to begin to affect change, at least in Western industrialized nations.

* * *

In the midst of these expectations and cultural limitations, I made the decision to try to continue my formal schooling.

Most of the other students who had finished their associate's degrees at Lakeshore Technical College were planning on continuing their education and their dreams sparked mine. But, how could I? The Comprehensive Employment and Training Act (CETA) would not cover my continuing costs and I couldn't afford to go on without help. But then it hit me, maybe there were other financial packages for earning a bachelor's degree. And there were. I qualified for student loans (which did not have to be paid back until after graduation), and a basic grant, which I would never have to pay back. I was learning that it definitely pays to ask. My credits transferred to Lakeland University, a few miles from where I lived, and it would only take an additional two years to get my bachelor of arts degree. I enrolled for the following semester.

Reflections

- What kinds of experiences lead to stepping beyond cautions or hesitations?

- The more I faced my fears the more fearless I was becoming.

- Have you ever had a godly vision? What did it feel like?

- Why was I such a slow learner when it came to men. Why did I have to wait until the pain exceeded the reward before I could, or actually would, move on?

CHAPTER 8
I MOVE ON
(1980~1982)

Never in a million years had I expected to be going to a four-year college.

My big dream had been to go to Central High, where my brother Bob had gone. The fact that few women from the 1940s era went to college made my being enrolled at Lakeland College that much more special. I wasn't taking anything for granted.

Sitting in silence on this campus was truly a blessing, watching birds in flight and squirrels squirming all around. Being on over 300 acres of campus land with well-manicured grass and beautiful flower gardens, and older brick buildings with high towers overlooking the campus in a prestigious manner, was all a delight.

I had decided to major in business administration, with a minor in psychology. The reason for psychology? I had to find what makes human's tick.

I loved being with younger students having in-depth discussions about life. In one class, the professor asked, "Is it okay for a man and woman, having just met at a wedding, to go to a motel for sex afterward?" Being a mom, I asked, "What if a younger child overhears this couple talking about their adventure and gets the message that having sex with a stranger is okay? What if a teenager, struggling with what's right or wrong based on parental teachings, overhears? Might an innocent young person make a mistake in life because of something they were too immature to handle?"

My life experiences were an asset in the class and led to deep discussions. I was accepted as one of the students, age difference or not, and ended up being given a high grade because of my participation.

I loved discussions about things like human masking and the literal ways beards or make-up give people something to hide behind. What do we fear? How do alcohol and drugs remove inhibitions? Why does body language and/or voice pitch change depending on the audience? What statements are made by standing tall or slouching. Psychology taught me to be aware.

So many college experiences focused on actual day-to-day life. Learning-disabled students progressing to living alone. Creating mock trials with students acting as jurors. Talking so openly about secrets and doubts I'd kept walled up inside me for so long. I kept asking, "Why don't we do this in public schools; learning about genuine living?" All of these lessons helped me continue growing forward, touching corners of life I would not have known about otherwise.

There were some basic skills I worked to advance. I got a C-grade on a first paper and talked with my teacher (who did increase the grade when I explained my primary source research strategy of interviewing my psychology professor, the editor of a local newspaper, and my fellow students). This was another lesson in speaking up for myself. He also said, "Diane, I think it would be best if you took the persuasive writing class next semester. It would help you with all your remaining classes."

I was not afraid to improve my skills. In the class, I wrote and rewrote paper after paper until they were right. I looked forward to the little notes the professor would put on each paper stating things like, "This was better, now you're getting it." On the final paper, I got an A- with margin note, "Can't believe it, this is damn-near perfect." Why the minus? A few spelling mistakes.

Ignorance is a very important word. I tell people I am ignorant, lacking knowledge in knowing the ways of the world and their meanings, but I am willing to learn. I'm not stupid or dumb, and neither are they or you.

One required course scared me to death: business law. Evidently, I assumed a person had to be super-smart to deal with the law, and I must not have seen me as that person. I ended up loving the class and got an "A" grade in it! Another positive lesson. You never know until you've tried.

I was so enjoying being at Lakeland College. One sunny day, I was outside talking with a professor of mine who was very pleasant to be around; always had a smile and ready to discuss life. Two other students joined us as I was saying, "Look to the sky, where does it end? I can't comprehend it, can you?" The four of us talked about the mysterious world we live in. I loved those kinds of deep discussions about life and the wonders of it all.

Several months later, I saw an advertisement for the college picturing the four of us talking. There I was, little Diane, on the cover of an educational advertisement for a college. Again, as I'm writing this, the tears are surfacing. *How did I ever make it so far? A miracle?*

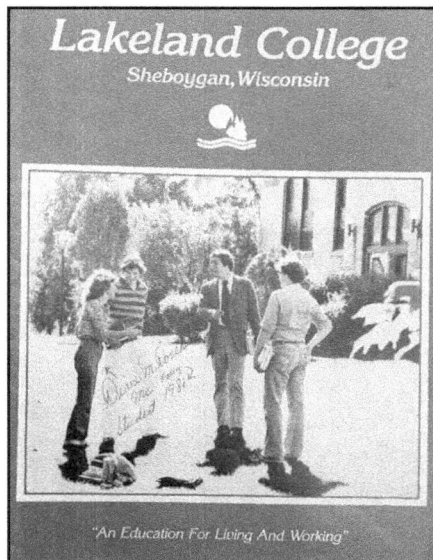

Lakeland College
Sheboygan, Wisconsin

"An Education For Living And Working"

And speaking of a miracle, there was an unusual happening while I was still in college. As I've mentioned, I had been attending St. Peter Claver Church since moving to the city. They were having a four-day mission renewal event being presented by monks wearing long orange-colored robes and sandals. I knew instantly I had to attend that event. I was hearing, for the first time, meditations concerning Jesus. If you recall, as a child, I had loved Jesus and cried for any pain he suffered.

In words—spoken in soft, low-toned voices—we were told to relax, to calm ourselves, to just be. We were guided by verbal images to a path leading toward someone sitting in the distance.

Swept up into the words, I became unaware of anything around me. As I imagined approaching the person sitting on a bench, under a sunlit tree, I found myself looking into the eyes of Jesus.

I was mesmerized and could only feel a deep love, a true love that cannot be explained in normal human words. The experience was very similar to the feelings and vision I'd had on my way to revisit Father Dave.

* * *

In May 1982, I graduated from Lakeland College and was given this referral by a favorite professor:

As a student, Diane combines an unwillingness to accept easy or pat answers to complex questions with a clear willingness to learn. She is a lively participant in class discussions, is prompt with assignments, and looks for additional, out-of-class opportunities to learn.

There was that *learn* word again. Learn, learn, learn. I was a student in the classroom of life.

But 1982 was not a good year to graduate. Businesses were not hiring; people were being laid off. I sent my resumes and made phone calls regularly. I re-contacted businesses on a weekly basis, figuring that if they got to know me my chances of getting a job would increase. My job was to keep looking for a job. I checked for work in other states and would have moved. The employment market was a no go. One manager I interviewed with told me to play it down. More than once I heard the words "over-qualified."

At a large local manufacturing firm, I applied for a management position in their transportation department. The interviewer told me he wanted to meet me himself because of the complimentary comments he had heard from the men who interviewed me for another position. That comment left me with a strange feeling, something like I was being looked at, like a male was eyeing me up.

In the interview, he continued talking about himself and his volunteer work. By this time, he had his feet up on his desk. What kind of professional attitude or behavior was that? Certainly not one of respect.

As we came to the end of the interview, he said, "You strike me as the type of woman who would allow a man to open a door for you."

"Of course, I would," I replied, "but if I arrived at the door first, I'd open it for him."

I did not get the job.

In the past, I would have felt inferior to this man. But my life experiences, schooling, paying attention, and becoming aware had now taught me that this man would suffer because of his attitude. Maybe someday he would awaken to, "Do unto others, as you would have them do unto you."

* * *

Due to the failing economy, Phillip lost the business we had started together and my child support stopped. The two older daughters had moved out of the household, but the two younger ones were still at home. So, what did I do? The only thing I could do—I applied for welfare.

Welfare helped when I needed financial support. At first, I didn't think too much of it, but as time went on, I became aware of friends saying, "I have to go to work tomorrow." I noticed that I was actually starting to envy them. It was like they had a purpose and I didn't. I was also becoming aware that it wasn't fun standing in line with food stamps knowing that people were watching. I didn't go to college to then live on welfare. I needed to do something, but what?

For 1½ years, I looked for work and finally settled for two part-time jobs working more than 40 hours a week, with no benefits. I helped start a small, one-person business making products for people with handicaps. It was literally a start-up business and I cleaned out a basement location, taking rusty and broken junk out to a dumpster. I swept cobwebs from the ceiling and corners, and painted the walls. I created a shelving unit, inventory, and purchasing system. The one-woman, do-all employee, that was me. The job was lonely, but it gave me a purpose and ended my welfare. In my second job, I stocked shelves and took care of customers at a long-time local retail store. Being around people was positive and it was good that job wasn't in a basement.

Then my daughter, Pam, called.

"Mom, a friend of mine told me there's a full-time underwriter position open at Heritage Insurance Company, on the south side of Sheboygan. The position includes a training program for entrance into the insurance industry. I thought you might want to apply."

I immediately contacted the company and talked with the head of Human Resources. I told him I already had an application on file from having applied a year ago. He said he needed an updated one, but I was a professional interviewee by this time and our phone call became my initial meeting. Before we hung up, my in-person interview was set for the following week.

I arrived at Heritage Insurance early, filled with excitement, but calm at the same time. Feeling good. This job, if I got it, would fulfill the dream I had of becoming a professional woman who wore a suit, high heels, and drove a company car. Thinking back, as a child, I had always loved sitting at a desk playing as though I was doing the important work of moving papers, opening drawers, taking out and putting back important items. Always organizing and pushing a pencil. I loved watching a pencil or pen as it left its mark on paper.

The interview went very well and the man who hired me proved to have a sense of humor and morals of respect. I liked him right away.

A week later, I was hired as a Personal Line's Underwriter: a full-time job as a professional wearing a suit, high heels, and that company car. The money was good and benefits too.

A dream come true.

Reflections

- What makes humans tick?

- What does it take to be open to improving skills and acknowledging you have more to learn?

- You never know until you have tried—where does the courage to try come from?

- Ignorance is a very important word. I tell people I am ignorant, lacking knowledge in knowing the ways of the world and its meaning, but I am willing to learn. I'm not stupid or dumb, and neither are they or you.

CHAPTER 9

A FULL-TIME JOB— WHAT COMES NEXT?

After seven years of schooling and searching, I was ready for my long-awaited career. Forty-three years old.

Monday, August 20th, 1984. I was nervous and excited for my first day on the new job. I wore a navy-blue suit with a complimentary silk blue-tone, rose-colored blouse. And my navy-blue high heels. My clean, curled hair was long but off my face. I felt professional as I walked towards the building entrance. Little did I know that my life was going to change in unusual ways over the next ten years.

The same inner voice that presented beautiful sunsets contrasted with ugly carcasses, and then Jesus' face imagined as I sat under a sunlit tree, now told me, "You are going to meet your future husband here." This seemed unlikely since I assumed men my age would be married with families and not looking for a wife.

Day one of my training, I met Sally. With the self-assurance that came from having a real job, at the first break, I offered, "Would you like to take a walk outside? The weather is so nice; the fresh air would feel good." She agreed. There were two men (Mark and David) standing outside who noticed us as we passed them. Were they future husband material, I wondered?

As time went on, Sally, Mark, David, and I became buddies, sitting together in the cafeteria. Mark was a tall and slender man with a warm personality. He was married. Sometimes we walked around the Heritage grounds, sharing philosophies about life. At times, I counseled Mark, in the same ways I had helped friends back in 7th and 8th grades. Only now I had more life experiences to share and draw from.

David was built like a football player, tall with broad shoulders and a slim waist. I didn't go on walks with David the way I did with Mark, so it took a little longer to get to know him. We would sit together at break once in a while. He was more private than Mark about his personal life, but very good at asking questions about mine. He was a jokester and always greeted me with a warm smile. I liked spending time with him.

David and Mark were partners in crime, doing things like sneaking birthday treats, when any were available.

* * *

Heritage Insurance Company trained me for three months to be a Personal Lines Underwriter (coverage on homes, vehicles, motorcycles, boats, and other personal items). Days, I was learning on the job and nights, I was studying for the INS21, Principals of Insurance exam, that covered the history of insurance, and more. I had insurance coming out of my ears and even started dreaming about it.

After the training, I joined the rest of the Personal Lines Underwriters in their fresh surroundings, filled with plants and sunshine. The people welcomed me with warm smiles. I liked it there. My main job was focused on the northwest region of Wisconsin, making decisions about granting insurance coverage, denying it, or canceling existing insurance. I was learning on the job, talking with agents, getting answers to their questions, and

passing the answers on. We both learned. Public relations was an important people-pleasing part of my job.

Questions were like, "Can an insured person drive their personal vehicle working at delivering a Domino's pizza, and still have coverage under a 'Personal Line'? What do you think? Nope. Delivery would be classified as business, not personal. That person would need commercial lines insurance coverage, or be canceled from the personal lines coverage if found out.

I was learning, learning, learning and getting better and better at my job as a result. And I got an E on my final INS21 test. E for Excellent! My 43-year-old brain still had more smarts than I had given it credit for. It was actually doing better than average work. Maybe being a little older wasn't so bad.

As time went on, I was enjoying training new underwriters coming into the department and working on special projects. Even though I had always said I never wanted to work in a restaurant or in insurance, I was enjoying my new career; I was a student in the classroom of life. Like that business law class I feared but ended up loving, I was feeling the same about my new career. Goes to show, you never know.

A Purpose-Driven Life

* * *

It was nearing Christmas when I found a white envelope in my office desk drawer. "Happy St. Nick, Ho, Ho, Ho," was written on the outside and a Hershey candy bar was inside. *Nice of the company to do that*, I thought.

But when I asked Sally and other co-workers about their candy bars, none of them had gotten one. Now we had a mystery on our hands. "Go ask Joe. I bet he put it in your drawer." (It was known that he liked me in a special way). "Joe, did you put this candy bar in my drawer?" "No." *Who did this? Could it be that future husband?*

Sally was determined to find the answer. She asked David, "Do you know who put that envelope in Diane's desk?" He seemed interested in the story but replied, "No I don't." Break was soon over, but as Sally and I walked away David called out, "Happy St. Nick, Ho, Ho, Ho." It was David.

But, wasn't he married?

Later, a co-worker who knew David well told me he had been asking about me. Turned out, he wasn't married.

Soon after that, David asked me out. I turned him down, I already had plans. A week later, he asked again and I turned him down a second time. I already had plans, and again, wasn't going to drop my plans for the sake of a date.

Over time, I got to know David better and decided I would ask him on a date. "Hi, I was wondering if you would like to join me and another couple going to a big band concert next month?" He said yes!

Our first date went well. David met my friends. We all enjoyed the music and went out for a drink after. Then David walked me to my door, said a few things about the night, then asked, "Is it okay if I give you a hug?"

Well, blow me away. I was not expecting that, but I welcomed it. It was a nice warm hug that had me on a cloud for a few days to come. Future husband? Time would tell.

David and I started dating and enjoying each other's company. After about three months, I asked, "How are you feeling about me?" There was silence and then, "I think I'm falling in love with you."

I cannot recall what was said after that, but knew that I too had developed feelings for him. I had been divorced for eight years and David for two years. I had four daughters; he had no children. We had not agreed that our relationship was exclusive. Then, coming out of a store, I saw David drive past with a woman in his car. The next time I was with him, I asked, "David, who was that I saw you with on Friday at about 7 pm?"

"An old friend."

"Have you been seeing other women when you and I aren't together?"

"Yes." He had been.

I felt quite hurt and angry, and said, "I will not be a number in your little black book. I'm not going to be one among many."

Based on that, he decided he was not ready for any serious commitment.

He had some thinking and growing to do. We were very compatible and loved doing things together. My energy was equal to his, even though I was 11 years older. What happened? Was it too soon after his divorce? Was it my daughters?

During the next four years, more than once, David would break up with me, and then get back together. I would shed painful tears. But even though this was happening, I felt we were meant to be together.

Well, during those next four years, it turned out I had some growing to do too. When David and I were apart, I would meet other men on the dance floor and this gave me the satisfaction of being around male energy, dancing, and having fun. I learned about different personalities and behaviors and what was expected of me as a woman and how I was treated. I was also realizing I still didn't have things under control when it came to men, even though I felt confident when it came to work and other responsibilities.

With David, I did not follow my own ground rules about not being a number in his little black book. I allowed him to come and go, making excuses for him. I had come so far, but not far enough where men were concerned.

Determined to stand up for myself, the next time David asked me out, I realized enough was enough. I said, "No, I don't ever want to see you again. You have hurt me enough!"

This caught him by surprise. "Oh, come on, let's go have some fun!"

"No!"

David had been in control of our on-again, off-again relationship. I finally got rid of the cobwebs from my past. The pain from the separations now exceeded the rewards of being together. I'd had enough and moved forward.

* * *

It was a Friday night when friends and I went out dancing. A group of guys came in, looking to have some fun, and one of them, Blake, asked me to dance.

He was tall and slim with light-colored hair. He was a wonderful dancer and fun to talk with. He told me about how he and his buddies had sailed to the Sheboygan Yacht Club to go to the June Sprint car races at the very famous Elkhart Lake Road America race track and see Indy cars, Mustang, classics, Can/Am, Trans Am, NASCAR and other races.

He asked for my phone number at the end of the night and called me the next morning. "Would you like to join us for the Road America races today?"

A Full-Time Job: What comes Next?

We all piled into their rental car, which meant I sat on Blake's lap. That was okay with me.

After the races, we drove into the village for the party time. As the six of us in the car were looking for a place to park, we were pulled over by the police. Our driver had crossed the line down the middle of the road, which was the reason listed. He was given a ticket. We all chipped in to pay the fine. Oh well, it came with the fun.

Sunday morning, Blake called again. "Diane, would you like to join us for breakfast before we head back to Michigan?"

"Oh, I would love to, but I have Becky to think of. I was gone all day yesterday." (Pam and Wendy no longer lived at home, and Dawn had other plans).

"Oh, that's no problem. Bring her along."

Becky, now 13 years old, agreed and off we went. She was treated like an old friend and was liking the attention too. Before they left to sail back to Michigan, they took us out for a cruise on Lake Michigan. The day was so perfect. Becky and I lay on the bow of the sailboat in the sun and watched the waves. What a wonderful and unexpected weekend it had been

Thinking back, if I hadn't faced my fears, if I hadn't worked at pushing myself forward, if I hadn't taken the time to learn, learn, learn, I would have missed out on a lot of fun things in life. I had been doing the work and it was paying off; happiness was presenting itself.

Reflections

- Do you have a small inner voice that speaks to you, and that you listen to?

- How do you face your fears? How do you push yourself? Are there things you feel you've missed out on because you were afraid?

CHAPTER 10

THE LARGER WORLD

It was time for an important life lesson. Growing up in Sheboygan, my lack of education and experience in the larger world, led to narrow thinking. I need to explain why it was so important for me to meet Black people.

To begin with, growing up, I don't remember seeing any people of color around me. That lack of experience—that ignorance—created fear in me. It played out in my thinking and my actions.

As you know, I was sent to live with my parents in Chicago in 1958. That was my first experience of seeing and being around Black people, or even so many people, all at the same time.

Mom picked me up at the train depot and we got on a bus to go to their apartment. As we passed a city park, I saw someone sleeping on a bench, which I thought was so funny and odd all at the same time. Out loud, I said, "Mom, look at that guy on the bench!" Mom nudged me to keep quiet. I couldn't help myself because I had never seen that in Sheboygan. It must not have been allowed in our town where Blacks had to literally be out-of-town by sunset.

Being on the bus enabled me to see tall buildings, clustered neighborhoods, shops, cars, and people walking everywhere. Riding the subway with Mom and Dad let me see people coming and going, getting on and off, rushing to beat the closing doors, people shoulder to shoulder. Everything was so new and I was absorbing it all.

Dad suggested we get off the subway and take a bus back home so I could see even more. Unknowingly, when we exited the subway, all the people walking and driving around us were Black. There were row houses with steps leading to the front doors. Black people were sitting and socializing on the steps. Lights flashed from several police cars.

We were uncomfortable, afraid, and at a loss; we felt like we were in a foreign land. We started walking to find a bus stop. People were friendly and probably sensed that we were lost, which our faces, body language, and energy would have spelled out loud and clear. A nice lady directed us to a bus stop but the bus did not stop for us. Nor did the next one. Why wouldn't the bus stop for us? Finally, Dad swung out his arm at the next bus and it stopped. We were told that buses and cabs only stopped when they were hailed.

As we rode the bus, I started searching for White faces. No White people. Black people were getting on and off the bus. I looked in store windows expecting to see White people working there, as though Black people weren't capable.

Out of this unknown space grew a huge amount of fear.

It is so hard putting into words what I was feeling. So lost. So afraid. I was an ignorant, sheltered, young person who had so much to learn about life and living. Without my knowledge—or agreement—small-town 1950s Wisconsin had programmed me to believe that Black people were not as good as White people. And it did that without my even knowing a Black person! (There was one Black student in one of my classes, but I never got to know him. The only thing I recall about him was a comment he once made, "I talk differently when I'm with White people." What was the meaning behind those words? That comment stuck with me; it wasn't quite clear to me why he would say that. Again, this showed my ignorance.) Discrimination.

While I was a student at Lakeland College, I finally got to know a person of color. We were waiting for a mutual friend and got to talking. Before we knew it, we were chatting like old friends. We shared family and life stories and, later, would sit together on campus whenever we could. We were always glad to see one another and I was learning I had no reason to fear Black people, or at least this one friend of mine.

One night when my friend, Sandy, and I were out dancing, a well-dressed, really tall Black man asked me to dance. We had fun and agreed to meet for a walk the next day. He was in Sheboygan on business. We walked and talked about life in general and his family. I enjoyed his company.

Another friend introduced me to Lionel Aldridge, the late defensive end for the Green Bay Packers, and a sports radio announcer. We visited him at his home. All had fun in his very large hot tub, and enjoyed having dinner together. Once, when he picked me up at home to drive me to our friend's home in Sheboygan Falls, I noticed people looking at us as we drove past.

I, of course, figured they were looking because they recognized Lionel.

"Lionel, I notice lots of people looking at us."

"That always happens when I have a White woman in the car with me," was his reply.

Wow, I was so naïve. I never gave that a thought. I was just enjoying being with Lionel, knowing we would soon be sharing fun again with mutual friends. We even tossed a football around, if you can imagine that. Remember I loved playing sports of all kinds as a kid.

Those were fun-filled days.

I was continuing to learn life lessons and have new experiences. Growing forward.

But more lessons were waiting for me. Eventually, I would be leading group tours to South America and visiting India. My world was expanding.

Reflections

- Do I ever judge people today? Yes, I do. Am I a perfect angel? I wish I were. Are you a perfect angel? I believe never judging is quite difficult, but seeking to be aware of our unconscious, unaddressed biases is a place to start.

- I once asked a couple of history professors, "What do you think of history books?" "We would burn them." "Why?" Too often they are slanted to the author's lens—*his computerized brain*—the writers' assumptions of what is real. (And, often, history is written by men, for men, and about men and boys. But the same is true for race. History is often written by Whites, reflecting their own experiences and viewpoints.) What does this mean for the rest of us?

CHAPTER 11
PATHWAYS

Work was going well. I was 47 years old and now actually had spare time for new growth. But what? Book stores called to me. They offered so many learning opportunities.

One day, a book spoke to me. *Dancing with Broken Bones* by the late David Swartz, who was pastor of the Dubuque Baptist Church, Iowa. He described the pains from a wounded heart as broken bones. His words remined me of my childhood love for going to church and my tears for Jesus. Unknowingly, I had pushed those wonderful feelings aside.

It was time for a renewal now and this book was the calling that re-opened my thirst for Jesus, his teachings, and the godly things I had left behind while searching for self. I was on a mission to find what was missing in my life. I've heard it said that once a person reaches their goal there's an emptiness—no longer is there something to work towards unless a new goal shows it face.

Since my divorce, I had made all new friends and was creating an entirely novel life. I had become part of a group of women who started taking long walks together once each week. We took turns deciding where we would meet and where we would walk. We called ourselves the "Walkie-Talkies."

We once followed our ears to beautiful piano music in the distance and met the musician who was delighted to play the songs we requested.

We followed our hearts to a group of puppies on a person's front lawn where we got to touch, hold, and love them.

We admired a Model-T Ford and asked the owner for a ride, which he was pleased to give us.

We went roller skating outside (which ended up with me in the ditch, on my belly). But it was great exercise and I mostly loved it. A writer for the local newspaper photographed and wrote the story of our group. We felt like movie stars. More learning. More growing forward.

Then came "Dances of Universal Peace," a program being offered at the First Congregational Church in Sheboygan. My friend Char and I joined that free-flowing, soft, gentle dancing. And then we learned about Pathways, a program that held Universal Environment Wellness Retreats.

Being in the natural world was a central Pathways theme: take care of the earth, the water, and all plant and animal life. Without this, we all perish. We were instructed to hug a tree while thanking it. Char and I did this, but felt foolish and we may have giggled then, but not anymore.

Prayer was also central. At one point, we stood in a circle around a man who talked about a problem he was dealing with and he asked the group to pray over him. Some people extended their arms in his direction. A few touched his shoulders. It was all about outspreading our loving healing energy to him. We did meditations silencing ourselves, combined with deep breathing, all devoted to health and healing.

I became even more aware of what Mother Nature had to offer, remembering my earliest memories of the rushing Sheboygan River. The theme of caring for the natural world was becoming a lifelong passion for me.

From this experience, my friend and I heard about the Sinsinawa Mound, formerly the motherhouse of the Sinsinawa Dominican sisters, and a retreat center.

At that time, they had a labyrinth, an ancient symbol of wholeness used in meditation and prayer as far back as the Middle Ages. We walked the path, listening to soothing music, curving in one direction and then another, while moving to the center. Walking, I felt like I was floating. I fell to my knees as I entered the center and experienced a deep feeling of love. Words cannot express.

Life was showing me yet another new path, just as the Labyrinth had, and the next place that called to me was the Wholistic Health Center, founded by Marianne Helm, and co-founder Reed Forbush, from the First Congregational Church in Sheboygan. The basis for their Center was the belief that a good relationship with God or a Higher Power (spiritual life) is vital to overall health through integration of body, mind, and spirit. I had to find out what that was about. This too seemed to be what I was needing.

I had started going to St. Peter Claver Church again and discovered they took yearly residential retreat groups to the Monte Alverno Center on the Fox River near Appleton, Wisconsin. It was seen as an oasis from the hectic world. Meals were silent. Statues of Jesus and the Virgin Mary were in the buildings and I was reminded of these symbols from my childhood.

My room was small with a twin bed, a very soft, comfortable rocking chair, and a small wooden table. Everything was squeaky clean. I loved the feel of the space.

Many times, each day, we gathered in the quaint little chapel for 15- to 20-minute spiritual talks. Franciscan Friars, in plain brown robes, sandals, and rope belts knotted three times—symbolizing the three vows of poverty, obedience, and charity—gave inspirational talks that were not like church sermons. The words *sin* or *sinners* were never spoken. What I do remember is how I was enthralled with the messages being given; I could have listened for hours to what they were saying, while feeling the words as they were spoken.

My previous life had been so full of hellish-type feelings and experiences. So, to be in a place of love, a place of quiet, a place where I could tune in to me, meant the start of finding the answers to my hunger for more growth. Before the weekend was over, I knew I would return.

And I did return. Sooner than I imagined. Other groups had silent retreats at the Center. I was surprised to find a priest there from New York, who did Hands-on Healing, which I had seen done on TV but did not believe. "Who were they trying to kid?" How much were those people being paid to fall to the floor?

Now I was seeing it first-hand. People would quietly tell the priest what they needed healing for. He would then place his hand on them and the person would fall to the floor.

I had to find out if these were true happenings, but what did I need healing for? *I was not in need of physical healing. Then it came to me, I was in need of finding this new way of spiritual healing, spiritual living.*

I told the priest about my quest for healing. He touched me and my body turned to rubber. I fought it, feeling the old me needed to stay strong—in control. It was mysterious, but I was still accepting what life presented to me. When I left, I again knew I would be back.

* * *

Peggy and I—someone I knew from our counseling group—remained friends. She called one day when she was struggling with something.

As she was talking, this guided imagery response came to me.

"Peggy, envision a huge field of daisies in all sizes and shapes—some straight and tall, some short, some bent,

some nearing the end of their lives, others just sprouting. Some of the daisies are light. Some are dark. Some are colorfully brilliant. Some are smooth. Some shiny or dull or drab. No two of them are the same. Among them, bees are busy pollinating so the plants might survive. Grow. Now see a heavy dark rain storm on one side of the field, with its moisture helping to create new birth; new growth keeping nature alive.

On the other side of the field see the sun shining. Out of the dark comes light—out of the dark comes rebirth. Out of the old comes the new. Both can be happening at the same time. If we stand back, look over the daisy field, we can see what nature is doing.

Now, see these daisies as people in all their shapes, colors, and sizes living through storms as they present themselves. Storms come and go and with their passing comes the light with its new growth, just as with the daisies and the bees as they do their work."

I was totally exhausted after giving Peggy this message. I had no idea where that came from. I was feeling the message as I was giving it to her.

Remember this message for now. It will re-appear again many years in the future, but in a most unusual way.

Reflections

• Have you ever created an entirely new life – a wonderful new type of life—for yourself?

• Have you explored the spiritual life in the ways I have described: embracing the natural world, walking a labyrinth, feeling the mind/spirit/body connections, sharing silent meals with others, sensing hands-on healing, or walking through a guided imagery experience? What did you feel? What did you learn? How were you changed?

CHAPTER 12
DAVID REENTERS THE PICTURE

It was a Friday in 1988, seven months after I had left David sitting on my front porch. I decided to call him. He was crying, he said, watching the movie *Out of Africa*, which had been our movie, our love story. After repeatedly being separated, the couple, Karen and Dennis, decide their places are with each other, but as Dennis is returning, his plane crashes. They will never be together.

David and I imagined ourselves in those dramatic roles. Separated, although there wasn't going to be a plane crash. David asked if he could see me. Since I had walked away from him, I was living life fully. I was dating two men and a third one had asked me out. I was in control of my life. I had grown and matured and moved forward in a way that felt strong and wonderful.

Still, I said yes to David's request. We met and talked and met a few more times. I continued to see the other men.

Did I still love David? Yes, I did. Did I enjoy spending time with him? Yes, I did.

While David and I had been separated, I went alone to various churches to experience the different ways people worship. This had been refreshing and good for my soul. People were openly receptive to my explorative journey.

One Sunday, David and I, with my daughter Wendy and her husband, attended St. Peter Claver Church. We were sitting in the front pew during communion, when an unexplainable, yet wonderful Godly-Divine occurrence happened. I experienced the entire congregation as One. Nothing else existed. I could still see each individual, but at the same time, we were not separated. It was as if I was mesmerized, hypnotized. I felt love bonded us all.

* * *

What was happening? Why had I started going from church to church asking what is the true meaning of life? As I shared earlier, I had such a strong love for Jesus as a child. As I grew older, I was living a life of growing, experiencing, and feeling love.

Why, on my way to revisit Father Dave, had I envisioned how life connects us with nature, surrounding us? Why had I experienced sitting with Jesus during a Mission Renewal meditation? Why had Char and I suddenly found ourselves dancing to angelic music at First Congregational Church? Why had I accepted Pathways offering meditating, praying, and hugging trees? What was the meaning of being presented with the Sinsinawa Labyrinth that took me to my knees? And then the daisy field message I had given Peggy. Where had that come from and why had I been so exhausted after our talk? Why did I seek out the spiritual silent retreats that felt like they were taking me, more deeply, into a space of love? Now there was no mention of sin or sinners as there had been when I was growing up. I was not a bad person. That message no longer sat right with me.

Now I was hearing only messages of a loving Presence or Holy Spirit. It's not just the words; it's in the loving, caring actions, and feelings. What I was learning, experiencing, and feeling was speaking truth to my heart, to my soul.

I didn't know it at the time, but there was more to come, and it came more and more as the years passed.

* * *

It was November of 1988 and David said, "Well, here goes. Will you marry me?"

"What did you say?"

He repeated his proposal again and I replied, again, "Would you say that again?" I wanted to make sure I was hearing him right.

The third time, he included the fact that he wasn't just marrying me, but including my four daughters in the proposal as well.

"Do you want to think about it?"

"No. My answer is yes! Should we wait to have a June wedding?"

"Why wait?"

After the proposal, I asked, "When did you decide to ask me to marry you?"

David replied, "Remember that day you and I went to St. Peter Claver Church with Wendy and her husband? Such a strong feeling of love came over me as I was sitting there. I had goose-bumps. I knew I wanted you at my side as my wife. It was then that I made up my mind."

And, in my mind, I recalled. *Remember, back when I started working at Heritage Insurance and that little voice saying I would be meeting my future husband there? That little voice was right— it was David.*

My daughters had gotten to know David well, over time and were so happy to learn he would be a part of their lives. David and I bought champagne and, with glasses in hand, went visiting special people to let them know about our marriage plans. All were surprised and pleased for us.

A Purpose-Driven Life

I wanted the things I had missed in my first marriage ceremony: a beautiful white dress that made me feel like a princess, a walk down the aisle with special flowers, photos, music, a reception with family present, and then driving around town beeping the horn like the traditional small-town custom with streamers and a *Just Married* sign on the car. David knew my history and agreed to everything and it all unfolded as I dreamed, other than a small photography glitch.

Because both David and I had been divorced, a Catholic wedding was out of the question, but I had a friend. Remember Reed Forbush, from the Wholistic Health Center and minister at the First Congregational Church? Reed performed our marriage on April 8, 1989 with family, friends and all the trimmings.

Isn't it interesting how we meet people who later play an important unexpected part in our lives?

That morning, the sky was cloudy and gray. Snow. That afternoon, the sun arrived and it couldn't

Wedding with David, 1989

have been a more beautiful Wisconsin spring day, not unlike that daisy field message I had created for Peggy. My daughters were my bridesmaids.

On our way to the reception, David and I sat in the backseat of his old car while our best man drove around town, honking, just as I had dreamed.

Family and friends surrounded us at the reception. David surprised me when he stood up and expressed his love for me and for our family and friends being there. Warm hugs, laughter, and merriment filled the day. There was love in the air and, at day's end, I felt married to David in a way I never had with Phillip. Was my first marriage a puppy love as well as an escape from abusive parents and foster parents? I was young and foolish and scared which is not a good combination.

Life certainly has a way of steering us in directions we don't always expect.

We honeymooned in Hawaii. But, we almost didn't because David forgot to put gas in the car. Racing to the airport the next morning, David saw the gas tank was on empty. In 1989, filling stations around us were not self-serve and did not stay open 24/7, so we held our breath until we spotted one. Was it open? The attendant had just arrived when we did and initially told us he wasn't ready to open the station for the new day yet. But, hearing our dilemma, he decided to add our purchase to the sales from the day before and we made the flight on time. On the flight, we sat so close to each other that the thinnest of hairs would not have fit between us. We were truly in love.

Kauai and Maui were fantasy worlds with waterfalls and sunsets, sandy beaches, and the bluest water. Hawaiian music, with the native dancing, is so special and different in its sounds and rhythms. Romantic I might also add. It was the perfect place for a honeymoon.

* * *

We lived in Sheboygan until Becky graduated from high school and then moved to David's house in Elkhart Lake, on five acres of land. Buddy, the dog we purchased from the Humane Society twice, moved with us. I gave the interior of the house a whole new look and one day, David turned to me and said, "Because of you, what was once a house is now a home." It was music, hearing those words as I continued getting used to being appreciated, something I had not experienced for a large part of my life.

Being with David, I could suddenly afford things. We were both working and married. Times were changing. David suggested we surprise Becky and purchase the horse she had lost during my divorce. Treca. We did and what a wonderful Christmas surprise that was for her. The *Sheboygan Press* ran a story on her gift. In part, it read:

> *Becky grew up living in the country on a hobby farm, and spent a lot of time playing with the dogs, cats, gerbils, and horses, among the normal thing's kids play with. She shared all of these things with her three older sisters, Pamela, Wendy, and Dawn.*
>
> *At age six, Becky's world was torn apart. Her mother and father got divorced. The country home, along with the animals was sold, including Becky's beloved Treca. Becky's heart was broken. I had to make it clear that we could not afford to keep Treca. She told me years later that she would sometimes cry herself to sleep at the loss.*
>
> *A very happy and surprised Becky now had her beloved Treca back with an additional unexpected gift—Treca was pregnant!*

Happy tears were shed that night. All Becky could say was, "You guys!"

DAVID REENTERS THE PICTURE

* * *

One day, Char called to tell me about a Milwaukee woman who taught meditation using guided imagery. Her program would run for eight weeks, one night per week. Char needed to say no more; I knew instantly I wanted to go. I thought it strange that I made up my mind so quickly as that wasn't normal for me.

The meditation class was held in a nicely decorated room located in a public building. There were various types of cozy chairs positioned in a circle. We could sit wherever we wanted. I noticed interesting pictures on the walls as I walked around getting the feel of the area.

The meditation was spiritual in nature. We were guided to see descriptive fields, paths, sunsets, rooms, nature, and people. The speaker spoke in soft soothing words of expressions, suggesting that we would eventually see our personal, spiritual guide. This was entirely new to me. At the end of each session people would share what they had felt during the meditation. They gave such glowing descriptions of their guides—something like a guardian angel. That is the best way I can describe it. I always came up with nothing or no one. I so wanted to feel what the others seemed to be experiencing.

You won't believe the following, but it's all true! It happened one night when Carol, the instructor, brought in the framework of a pyramid. Spiritually, the pyramid is highly symbolic, representing the physical body. The sides are the journey of life and the point symbolizes union with one's higher power. In the Christian tradition, the triangle represents the Holy Trinity of Father, Son and Holy Spirit as well as faith, hope, and charity.

On this particular night something was different. As I was sitting with almost my entire legs completely inside this large pyramid, and as the meditation started, I knew what was going to be said BEFORE the words were spoken. I saw images of people and landscapes BEFORE they were being described in the meditation. I saw me carrying a cross down or along a path. I then saw someone else carrying it. In my imagination, we turned into a large grassy field of burning candles. It was beautiful. I knelt before my guide, and as I looked up, I discovered it was Jesus on the cross. Was Jesus being my guide a surprise? At that instant? Yes. I can't explain how that felt knowing ahead of time what was coming, and then seeing Jesus. But then my having had him deep in my soul as a young child already, who else could possibly be my guide?

A week passed since I first saw Jesus as my guide. Char and I arrived early at meditation class so I could spend time looking at the unusual paintings on the walls that I had seen the first week we came.

I asked Carol, the meditation instructor, about the unusual paintings. She replied, "The artist takes people's names and birthdates, meditates on them, and then paints the image that comes to her and writes the message on the back of the painting. She happens to be here tonight; she's sitting right over there. Her name is Kristy."

What? That was the first night Kristy came, she hadn't been there the past five weeks. Was it a coincidence she came the night I took serious interest in the paintings?

I approached Kristy with enthusiasm. I was definitely interested.

"Could a picture be done for me?" I asked.

"Yes, will you be here next week?"

"Yes, I will."

When I got there the following week, Kristy told me that she didn't have the finished product, but she had a pencil sketch and the message.

"Would you like to see it?"

Oh, my God, the picture was of a large field filled with lots and lots of daisies, with the painting being very dark on one side of the field and very bright on the other side, like I had described in the message I had given my friend Peggy, many years before. Remember, Kristy knew nothing about the message I had given Peggy.

The message on the back of the picture was, "I think the most prominent are the sunflowers. (*Kristy, not knowing the message, thought the daisies were sunflowers—they look alike.*) Out of the dark comes birth. All the green represents new growth, and yellow is inspiration—learning. The seeds also represent birth. (*In the painting the seeds look like rain as they are falling down from the flowers.*) And if you look closely, you may see other symbols,

Daisy field spiritual painting

like bees. There seemed to be birds in the white, which is the messenger. And also, *the guide* to continue spreading the message to many."

One thing she added, front and center in the picture, was a woman and a small child, each sitting on a large daisy. They were looking over the daisy field watching nature as it teaches us the lessons in life if we only pay attention—people as daisies—Life.

David was already in bed when I got home that night. I was too excited to wait until morning to tell him what had happened. I woke him up. "David, you won't believe this. The picture and message from Kristy hold the same wisdom I gave Peggy a number of years ago!"

Blow me out of the water—how could that be? I started giving spiritual paintings to people after that. They were always surprised how right-on the paintings and messages were.

* * *

For five years in a row, Char and I traveled to New York City to attend Omega Workshops, which focus on awakening the best of the human spirit by being interconnected and responsible for each other and the earth. The holistic workshops were organized into six categories: body, mind, and spirit; health and healing; creative expression; relationships and family; leadership and work, and sustainable living. Char and I came home refreshed and more inspired each time. I was learning how protected I had been living in little Sheboygan, Wisconsin. There I was—that little girl who thought she'd never get out of Sheboygan—but life was proving me wrong. Going to those workshops gave me the opportunity to meet people from all over the world.

My path into questions on the meaning of life continued and David joined me in the journey. We attended a three-day Deepak Chopra seminar that focused on his themes of ageless body, timeless mind, quantum healing, and perfect health, ridding ourselves of fear, and more. Chopra was using ancient wisdom and modern science to open the mind and feed the spirit and he stimulated us to new ways of thinking and examining life.

Now I was on a roll. What is life about? What is there about life I don't know? What more is there for me to learn? How can I help others? How can I share what I have learned because of my life experiences?

I was noticing books and magazine articles about life and living that I never paid attention to before. Because of the unusual happenings I'd already had in life, I was now pushed to finding answers to mysteries that didn't make sense with my old ways of thinking. I wondered, *What or who is God?* I started looking for and listening to any and everything I could about Jesus. *I had to know more about the Spiritual World.* I had to find the truth. *Find the Truth and The Truth Will Set You Free.*

* * *

It was 1994. I called my friend Peggy asking if she would like to go to the Retreat Center with me. She had never been there and after hearing what I had to say, she said, "Yes." I looked forward to going again, I hadn't been there in quite some time.

The weekend was proving to be full of love feelings as always; such an inspirational place to be. As I was sitting alone in silence in the chapel, I heard that little voice again. This time it wasn't so little and the message was very clear, *Quit Your job. I have other things for you to do!* There was no mistaking it, the message was VERY clear.

I told Peggy about the message. I didn't know what it meant, but I knew what I had to do.

David was sitting in the backyard when I got home. I approached him, "David, I have to quit my job." I told him about the message I heard while in the chapel. After knowing all the other unusual growth experiences I had been having the last few years, this didn't seem to surprise him. He was okay with it. Three weeks later, I was out of my job. Just like that.

* * *

Where is life taking me, I wondered. The world I was experiencing was already mysterious to me. What new experiences could be waiting for me? What is my purpose?

Bittersweet experiences. That was what awaited me.

I stopped to visit Mom at her apartment and saw something I had never seen before. Remembering the look in her eyes still brings tears for me. After I woke Mom up, she needed help walking. I suddenly realized that the person who had always been strong, who had kept working and held things together for Dad, was now extremely weak and fragile. Although she never complained, I now saw that she wasn't made of steel. She was flesh and blood, a person with feelings and needs like other humans.

We had always assumed Mom would move to Sunny Side Nursing Home toward the end of her life but when I talked with her about it, I could see by her facial expression and the tone in her voice that she really didn't want to go there. So, I went to take a look at the place. People were sitting in wheel chairs, slumped over. They had no expression on their faces and it seemed so cold and lonely.

Still, this was not an easy decision for me. I continued to feel anger towards my mom because of the way I had been treated by her and Dad. Now, seeing her at her weakest, I realized it was time for me to forgive. This is where words cannot express where decisions come from—those feelings and emotions from deep within one's being. I realized I loved Mom no matter what her faults. After all, I have faults too, but don't tell anyone I said that.

"David, I went to the nursing home today and didn't like what I saw. Are you agreeable to having Mom move in with us?"

As he had with me quitting my job, David accepted this change too.

We rented a hospital bed for her and made sure she had her favorite living room chair. She settled happily into the larger of our two bedrooms.

How does a couple adapt to having a parent move in? Well, I decided it would be the time for a trip. Las Vegas of all places. Remember that Mom was always a party person, so Vegas was her dream. She was really excited about the idea, and recognizing she was dying, smilingly said, "This will be my last trip going anywhere." I can still hear her saying that.

Once in Vegas, we went straight to the slot machines. At 2 a.m., we had to pull Mom off the machines. She was having so much fun gambling and people watching. We took Mom, in a wheelchair, to see the sights the next day. She decided she wanted to walk a little, so suggested that David sit in her wheelchair while she pushed him. That lasted a short time. She weighed under 100 pounds and David was close to 200 pounds. Can you imagine what some people thought when they saw that? I have to smile when I think of that scene now. It was all a wonderful dream that she never expected. I love it when I can do fun unexpected things for people, it fills my heart.

* * *

Back home, we settled into a routine. Mom was so frail that I could carry her, and did. I gave her medications, bathed her, did her laundry, fetched things for her, and tucked her in every night, arranging the pillow and blankets just the way she wanted. She got hugs from David and me every night.

Once, when I was carrying her to the living room, she was holding on to the back of my neck as I turned sideways so we could pass through the doorway. She looked into my eyes and said, "Oh, sweetheart." Joking. She never lost her sense of humor.

Another day, I asked if she was afraid of dying. She said she was. We had a good talk about death, the unknown world, and what happens after we die. It was then that I gave her permission to let go, to pass on. It seemed like she needed to hear that it was okay to go.

I called Father George to come to see Mom. He was from a church closer to us that we attended once in a while. He agreed to come. He was a large man with a voice that rumbled. Mom was lying in bed, motionless, when Father George walked to her side. She looked up at him and he said, "Come on, get up, get out of bed. Let's go to the corner bar and have a couple." It seemed he intuitively knew what made Mom feel good and I know that, if she could have, she would have gotten out of bed and gone with him.

Mom died on August 7th, 1994. That morning, I found her motionless, but still breathing. I lifted her arm. It was limp. I knew she was dying but maybe she waited for me that morning. We had bonded as she was dying and all was forgiven, even though she hadn't learned to say, "I love you" or to give hugs. In her 70s, Mom did sign one card, "Love, Mom." That single memory still brings tears. Emotions run so deep.

I went off by myself right after her death and let the tears come as I knew they would. Dad had died 16 years before Mom. She was alone with him as he stated his final wish that his kids could have been there with him. It's such a strange feeling after someone passes, knowing they will never come back. Bob and I were orphans. (Bob was to die five years after Mom, in 1999.)

I called hospice and the nurse came right over. I stayed at Mom's side all the while. After the hearse drove away, I sat on the front porch and then told David I'd like to go for a short ride. We did, but then went right to work cleaning out everything that had belonged to Mom. Having her live with us during the last days of her life, plus the in-depth conversations about living and death, allowed me to let go. At the funeral, I was happy for Mom and did not shed a tear. I even thought, "Mom, you should be here, we're having a party for you."

Reflections

- Have you ever forgiven someone? What allowed that to happen?
- Have you ever needed to become the parent to your parent? A change of roles. Why did you do that?

CHAPTER 13

WHAT COULD POSSIBLY BE WAITING FOR ME?

Mom was gone and we had made peace between us before she died. I now reflected back on the message I had gotten at the Retreat Center, that little voice that very clearly said, *Quit Your job, I have other things for you to do!*

Well, I did *other things* when I took care of Mom. But now what?

In a brochure I happened to pick up, I saw information on Blake Long, a seasoned and recognized expert of holistic medicine, homeopathy, ayurveda (an ancient Indian holistic healing system), and yogic sciences, along with meditation, breathing techniques, and skillful living. This spoke loud and clear to me and David, so we decided we would take the 14-week program.

And that program, based in the work of Swami Rama who had founded the Himalayan Institute in Pennsylvania, led me (David did not go along) to Rishikesh in northern India. The group I was with stayed at Swami Rama's ashram—a spiritual hermitage for Indian religions—on the Ganges River. We walked in the Himalayan Mountains and visited temples that were thousands of years old. We participated in ancient rituals and experienced local culture with spiritual advisers. What would my life have been like, I wondered if I had been born in northern India?

* * *

Life continued to change. I now knew I needed to reengage in local issues. I attended a meeting to discuss domestic violence. I had lived this. There I met Pam Warmer, who managed a center for domestic violence against women. She spoke forcefully. "Something has to be done to stop abuse!" After the meeting, I briefly told her my story and then said, "I'd like to attach myself to you. I like what you have to say and the energy you have for doing something to help women."

This was my new path, my new purpose.

Pam and I worked through the Mental Health Center, which established the Sheboygan Area Family Enrichment Network (SAFE). It was a coalition of child advocacy professionals and volunteers working to reduce child abuse.

We participated in *Court Watch for Abused Children*. We went to court trials, involving child abuse cases, to let the judge and lawyers know there were two extra sets of eyes and ears observing how the trials were being led.

A local group was being formed for innocent men accused of sexual abuse of a minor.

I told Pam how excited I was at the idea of getting men to join the women to help stop child abuse. I believed men would listen to other men and maybe even shame them into seeing the wrongs of child abuse. Man-to-man sort of thing. Pam's reply was, "Diane, it would be a waste of time."

I responded, "But I have to at least try. I will go alone if I have to. I feel so strongly about it!"

Pam agreed to go, but repeated, "It will be a waste of time."

There were about 20 couples at the meeting, and one single man. Pam and I were a little out of place, but determined to ask them to join us.

Each man spoke, complaining about being accused of something he had not done. A few of the girlfriends or new wives spoke too.

When they were done, I raised my hand and started telling them why Pam and I were there. Before I could finish, it was as though the roof had caved in.

Everyone in the room turned on us and started yelling profanities in pure anger. They were cussing out their former wives and the very idea of helping women in any way. Even the women there were yelling and defending their men. In no way were they going to hear the entirety of what I was wanting to suggest.

Pam and I didn't feel real safe walking to the car that night. There was still anger in the air. We quickly locked the car doors.

Wasn't it interesting that anger, if the men were innocent, was stronger than the will to help young children?

Continuing our work, Pam and I went to hear Carolyn Myss speak. Little did I know my life was about to change again.

Carolyn Myss brought a guest speaker with her that day—Ron Roth. Ron had been a Roman Catholic priest for 25 years but left the priesthood because he could no longer live the church's teachings. He started his own church, "Celebrating Life."

When he spoke, it was like he was speaking directly to my heart and soul about religion, God, the Holy Spirit, the Divine, and the Creator, or the unseen world. It was like the fog had been lifted and I could see clearly why I loved the messages of Jesus. It was all about love, caring, giving of self, and forgiveness. He had a strong believe that we are all one and should treat others accordingly. He taught all this with a wonderful sense of humor that would often have us rolling in the aisles. I have such wonderful, fond memories, including "The Golden Rule in Ten of the World's Great Religions," which you can read in the Appendix.

A Purpose-Driven Life

* * *

I invited David to come with me to hear Ron speak in Chicago. It was David's first time interacting with Ron's ideas.

David, too, felt Ron's words in his heart and soul. As we came out of the session, we got information on Ron's upcoming retreat in Arizona. Without thinking about it, David said, "Let's sign up to go."

We were hooked and subsequently went to many of Ron's gatherings. We were learning about what we felt was the truth.

Church could no longer hold us in bondage to ancient teachings about the God world, the unseen world.

I found myself having a burning desire to help others more than ever. That little voice that had guided me through many years of growth was talking clearly. It was time to get serious about creating a way and means to help others, especially women who need some sort of guidance—a way of helping them to grow forward. Men needed to be educated right along with the women if everyone was to be on the same page in this *classroom of life*. The education had to be different, but how would I do this?

I started reading non-fiction and was learning new ways of thinking as a result. I attended seminars of all kinds, listening to well-known speakers like Deepak Chopra, Wayne Dyer, Marianne Williamson, Dr. Andrew Weil, Neale Donald Walsch, Ron Roth, Jon Kabat-Zinn, to list only a few. So many more messages were coming to me, I found out I needed to keep pen and paper by my bedside and in the car. Silent messages were coming rapidly.

One morning I was writing down a message so fast that I could hardly read it. I noticed it was different somehow. It didn't seem to fit with the rest of my morning inspirations. When it was finished, I gave it to my daughter, Wendy, to type and save on her computer for me. (I wasn't computer savvy at the time.)

124

A few weeks later, she called me to say, "Mom, my minister is looking for a woman to give the sermon for *Women's Sunday* this coming week. Would you want to do that using the paper you wrote and gave me to save?"

"What do I know about giving a sermon?"

"Well, give him a copy of that message and see what he thinks."

I gave the sermon for both services, that following Sunday, on that paper I had been inspired to write while having my pillow propped one morning. Wow, who would have thought?

A number of people on their way out of church that Sunday asked if I did counseling. They must have liked what they heard. This was a good thing.

* * *

Another book that impacted my thinking and awareness was Patricia Lynn Reilly's 1995 book, *A God Who Looks Like Me: Discovering A Woman-Affirming Spirituality.* Once I started reading it, I couldn't put it down.

What I read was filled with poetry, ritual, story, meditation, and history. It spoke of patriarchal images of early experiences that wounded women (and men too in the process) and stood in the way of a self-defined spirituality. It spoke of women in search of a woman affirming spirituality that reclaims their lost power, autonomy, sexuality, wisdom, and divinity.

This book was an eye-opener. As a child, I had always been asking, "Why?" I think I drove my mom insane. (Maybe that's why I got those slaps aside the head once in a while—just kidding.)

I questioned things like the treatment of women. I needed to know the why and how of it all. My ex-husband once told me that I was never satisfied.

An article dated July 27, 1995, in the Catholic Herald addressed some of my questions. A priest had written, "Few would fail to admit that there are problems with *father* language for God. We don't always have to refer to God in masculine terms as he. One problem is literally taking references to God as *he* or as *father* as meaning that God is a man, a male being. This is a none-too-subtle form of idolatry. God is not a man, not a creature at all, and hence neither male nor female."

Then, I came across two books: Uta Ranke-Heinemann's *Eunuchs for the Kingdom of Heaven: Women, Sexuality, and the Catholic Church* and Karen Jo Torjesen's *When Women Were Priests: Women's Leadership in the Early Church and the Scandal of Their Subordinati*. These books speak of the historic roots of the church's prejudice against women. The facts are researched and can be checked. It almost makes one sick learning how backward the thinking was years past, and parts of it are still influencing many people to this day. It's not just the Catholic Church where men have made the rules. It is spelled out throughout history.

And another book, Jenny Cockell's *Across Time And Death: A Mother's Search for Her Past Life Children*, left me thinking about that little voice that has guided me through life with my unusual visions and messages. There are things that happen that are out of the ordinary and cannot be rationally explained. Cockell's book tells of a woman who died and was reborn in another time. She had five children and died giving birth to her sixth child. As she was dying, she worried that the father would not take proper care of the children.

After her reincarnation, starting at a very young age, she kept drawing pictures of certain buildings for no known reason. As she got older, names started coming to her. She had dreams that spoke to her of people and places. She was having a sense of something from the past. Her husband, in her current life, encouraged her to do research based on everything she was experiencing. What she found were documents of all kinds listing names, locations, her death, marriage, and more from her prior life. Through those she was able to find the church she knew so well along with other places. And, she found her prior children who were still living, now in their eighties. (Pictures of the children, the documents, and her drawings are all in the book.) The children believed her to be their mother because of the things she knew, the things she now remembered. Was this a true story? Is there such a thing as a prior life? Is reincarnation possible? Can a soul be reborn in a new body?

And what is the meaning of all those visions and messages I have received over time? Quit Your Job. The Daisy Field. The We Are One vision I had in church. Unexpectedly giving a sermon at Wendy's church. The list goes on. All of these were out of the ordinary, at least according to how we were taught to believe.

Reflections

- Is it a positive thing never to be satisfied? Never to settle for less than you want? Why or why not?

- Have you ever met a human that felt like a God, the Holy Spirit, the Divine, or the Creator? What happened?

- Is there such a thing as a prior life? Is reincarnation possible? Can a soul be reborn in a new body? How can we know?

- What, if any, unexplainable experiences have you had?

CHAPTER 14
MY EVOLUTION CONTINUES

I was learning that unless I lived and experienced life fully, I could not help people because I wouldn't truly know their pain. People could tell me what fire feels like, but I have to put my finger in it to really know what they are talking about. Having lived the life I had was like me sticking my finger in that fire. I have a feel, not just book knowledge or someone telling me about their pain, but an inner knowing. A been-there, done-that sort of thing.

Those morning messages and notes I wrote resulted in a manual and then in an entire class, *Happiness Comes from Within*. I could have walked right into a classroom and taught from the collection of my messages.

I didn't know what to do with the manual and the class I had developed but then I was sharing my story with a person who said, "Take it to the university in Sheboygan. Maybe you could share or teach it there."

I thought about what she suggested and got up my nerve. I faced my fears and presented it to the University of Wisconsin–Sheboygan. They sent it on to University of Wisconsin–Madison for final approval. I was suddenly teaching my first class of 20 continuing education students. Now I knew why I had been inspired to take the course with Dale Carnegie, which taught me how to speak before groups.

The *Happiness Comes from Within* class was offered each semester from 1995 until 2001.

The promotion for the class read,

> *Happiness Comes from Within.*
>
> *This will be a discussion/workshop/support group that helps explore new possibilities for positive growth and happiness through self-awareness. Exercises will focus on identifying and avoiding self-defeating behavior.*

Those 20 students found the jokes with pictures I had placed on their desks each week because laughter is exceedingly important in a healthy healing way. You can't ever laugh too much. How do I know? *Experience.* Depression made me feel dead and was exceedingly painful. Laughter made me feel alive. During counseling I slowly remembered that as a child I played hard and laughed a lot. I wanted to laugh again. Then I stumbled on article after article that showed what I already knew—the importance of laughter. This was one of the topics we talked about as the weeks went on.

The classes were NOT the usual run of the mill. I started by having people put plastic bags over the top of their torso with holes cut for their arms and neck, and a paper grocery bag over their heads, with a small circle cut out so just the eyes, nose, and mouth showed. I wore the bags too. We all looked very much alike and it left an impression.

A good discussion always followed on how horrible it would be if we all looked alike, always dressed alike, had the same likes and dislikes, and all wanted to work at the same jobs. How boring.

We talked about how we were all basically looking for the same thing—happiness and contentment on the inside—but were simply coming from different directions as we acted out our learned beliefs and behaviors.

The first week I instructed the students to create a collage using only magazine pictures that made them feel good, with emphasis on *feel good*. At the end of those six weeks, students would share their collages and the reasons for the pictures they chose. One of the students, someone I knew from my insurance job, had gotten a Spiritual Painting, which he brought in to share as his collage. As a result, I shared my daisy field story with the students and told them how they could get a spiritual painting if they wanted to. The spirit world entered my *Happiness Comes from Within* class teachings from that night forward. Yes, life has a way of steering us.

As I continued teaching the class, I was also gaining more confidence in the message it contained. The students' responses, in my mind, were telling me to keep going, keep learning, and keep sharing my own life experiences. They commented on how the concepts presented were down to earth. They liked the broad spectrum of possibilities that did not necessarily follow societal norms. They felt the relaxed atmosphere let them ask why they were the way they were as they examined their inner selves.

* * *

The course expanded when Marianne Helm, founder of *The Wholistic Health Center*, asked if I would consider teaching there. When I asked what made Marianne think of me, she replied she was coming up blank on who could teach but then the answer came. She asked Reed Forbush, who had already passed on, and in her dream, he said, "Ask Diane Pauly." She didn't know that I had already been teaching the *Happiness Comes from Within* course.

As a result, I taught various versions of my happiness class, a *Circle of Wisdom* course, and numerous other programs from 1998 through 2001.

I developed a course on psychotherapist/teacher Judith Duerk's book, *Circle of Stones—Woman's Journey to Herself*. In 1999, the *Plymouth Hub City* newspaper ran a full-page story, with my picture, on the class. Judith agreed to personally present her retreat to the women I had gathered. She and I stayed in regular contact for six years after that. She asked questions about how a person's life might have been different if you had had a place where you could go to be just with women. And then she challenged women to join a circle to honor the feminine within ourselves; to feel alive by reclaiming their lives moment by moment.

* * *

2000: David and I went to a hearing put on by the Sheboygan County Conservation Congress on dove hunting.* There were angry words, or wise-cracking men, all around us, spouting how they were determined to get what they wanted—to be able to kill doves. The energy in the room was raw; the men wanted to have permission to kill these tiny birds.

My Letter to the Editor about the dove hunt was printed in the *Sheboygan Press*. I challenged all hunters who voted yes to killing doves to pick up a book, to read articles, to go to environmental centers, to become aware of what we humans are doing to our magnificent earth and what hunters are wanting to do to our beautiful doves. I ended with:

* The Conservation Congress is supported by the Department of Natural Resources. It is unique to Wisconsin and holds an annual Spring Hearing for the public of each county to provide input on a wide array of natural resources-related questions and submit resolutions for the public to consider.

MY EVOLUTION CONTINUES

There comes a time when we have to stop taking. There comes a time when we need to start giving back. We must think beyond ourselves.
Concerned for all of us, Diane M. Pauly.

* * *

My passion for protecting the earth had been part of me since those earliest days when I played by the waterfalls in Sheboygan Falls and ran through fields of flowers. Now I marched at the courthouse. I spoke in the city park and at the airport. It wasn't just the doves I fought for, but for ALL of Mother Earth's inhabitants, or we will not survive.

That little voice within was now pestering me to rent a billboard for my message: *We are so busy acquiring things of the world...that we have forgotten how to live. In the lower right-hand corner was a dove proffering the words: Love, Peace.* And my second billboard, years later, offered the words: *Be Kind to Everyone—Happiness Will Follow—Change your thinking, change your world.* The dove's words? *Love/Peace*

* * *

We are so busy acquiring things... of the world that we have... Forgotten how to live.

Change Your Thinking
Change Your World

Love
Peace

2002: David took a different job in Madison, Wisconsin.

But before moving to Madison, I returned to the circle where I had sat with the beautiful group of women when I needed counseling. To a degree, they helped save my life during and after my divorce back in 1977. This time, there were different women in the circle in need of help and guidance. I shared my story with them. As I left, I felt good knowing I had come so far and was maybe able to shine some light on their futures. I let them know there was hope if they faced their fears and got help when needed.

* * *

2003: David and I were still attending Ron Roth's gatherings, called *Intensives*. Ron shared a story of having been in Abadiânia, Brazil, to witness and experience the miraculous healings that were being performed there by João Teixeira de Faria, known as John of God. Ron said, "I felt like I had gone home."

João performed visible or invisible surgeries for physical ailments as well as other things like depression, alcohol abuse, marital problems, and emotional problems of all kinds. If a person chose an invisible surgery, which was preferred by most people, they could actually feel something painless inside themselves. For visible surgeries, João did not wear gloves and there were no pain pills. People stood during the entire time of the surgery, which took only a few minutes.

None of what I was hearing was ordinary by any means. I had to know more.

A friend, who is an optometrist, saw João do a scraping of the eye. Yes, scraping of the eye, which João said has many healing effects on the body. He used an ordinary kitchen paring knife. According to the optometrist, the eye was actually being scraped and there's no way humanly possible the pain could be tolerated under normal conditions. I personally saw this type of surgery being done a number of times, but never up close.

João said, "I do not heal anyone; the one who heals is God."

I purchased João's book, read it, and gave it to my daughter Becky to read. Becky's reaction was, "Mom, we have to go to Brazil." We were there from July 14 to July 27, 2003. My daughter, Dawn, and friend, Peggy, went with us.

Ron was right. The energy there was filled with love. People were asked to wear white when going to the Casa, which was where the gatherings and surgeries/healings were performed. Seeing people coming to the Casa all in white left an impression of coming together as one, while seeking healings of all sorts, looking for guidance, restoration, and love.

The stories and healings I heard about could have been unbelievable, except for the fact that I too had deep personal in-depth experiences. I was loving the calm rolling land, the softening natural sounds, and the silence of people meditating or speaking quietly to one another about that day's miraculous healings. It all felt so right.

I found myself talking out loud to my dad one day as I was slowly strolling down a dirt path, by myself, which led to the healing waterfall. But why was I talking to him now? Dad had died in 1978, 25 years prior. I had been so angry with him when he died that I never shed a tear.

I started thinking of how I was sharing my life story with people when I was teaching or lecturing at various events. "Sorry, Dad, I never asked permission to share our story." Then while thinking of our story and my dad, I said out loud, "I forgive you."

"And I forgive you," was a reply that came back at me out of nowhere, in the silence, but it was clear as clear could be. There was no mistaking it, I knew it was Dad. I knew it in the deepest depth of my soul. At that instant, I released the anger; I couldn't hold on to it any longer. The tears I had held back suddenly came all at once. After 25 years, Dad and I were at peace.

Another happening I can't explain occurred. I was told, "*You have to get a massage by this man. His massages are not ordinary.*" I was not a massage person, but from what I was hearing now, I figured I'd give it another try.

It's really hard to explain what happened during that massage. It was like a meditation and intense massage at the same time. I found myself slowly drifting into a most relaxing energy. It was like my mind and body were saying, *Thank you.* As I was taken in by this in-depth feeling, I felt a third hand placed softly on my forehead—Yes, a third hand. I was aware of it, but not frightened. How could this be? I knew exactly where his other two hands were. There was no one else in the room. Maybe there was an attachment somehow under the table? Would that be possible? I was left alone in the room afterward and I checked under the table. No attachment. I have no explanation, but I do know for sure, I felt a soft third hand.

Wait, there is more to this story. As I walked outside after the massage, a man and women were talking to someone. I acknowledged them with a smile and continued on my way. The following day, as I was walking toward the Casa, that same couple approached me and said, "We just have to tell you that we could feel you, we could feel your loving energy when you passed us yesterday." They felt compelled to tell me about it.

I shared a room with Peggy. Becky and Dawn were next door. One night, Peggy and I heard a rapping on the wall. We figured we were being too loud, so we turned out the lights and went to sleep. The next morning, Peggy and I apologized to the girls for keeping them awake. Becky and Dawn said, "We didn't hear any rapping on the wall. You didn't keep us awake." That was a mystery to me until I picked up a new book. Something in me said to look in the back of the book, which I did. What I saw was the clue that spirits will, at times, rap on a wall. It was a strange, but interesting, experience.

And another unexplainable experience happened as Peggy and I were talking in our room when an intense very strong love feeling swept over me. I could feel it deep within me to the point that it was hard for me to speak. I asked Peggy if she was feeling it. She said she could feel it in the room, but not in her body. I can't explain what happened that day, but I have had that happen once in a while since then. It seems to happen when I'm teaching or talking about love, caring, and giving. It's almost like something or someone takes over.

* * *

Because of the experiences I was having, I felt David needed to go to the Casa too. He agreed. And it's a good thing he did. He became my banker for the following reason.

David and I had joined the Unity Church and I figured that would be the perfect place to share my experiences from the Casa in Abadiânia. I was right. What I didn't plan on was being asked to be the travel agent for subsequent trips. I set up flights, helped with visas and passports, handled their money, and, in Abadiânia, even counseled people.

In the morning, the travelers met João for a few seconds, and were then instructed to go to the healing waterfall or the extremely relaxing healing crystal beds. At 2pm, they returned for their surgeries. In time, they became part of about 200 people sitting and meditating in the Current Rooms. People asking for healing would walk through those rooms to stand before João. Interpreters translated for people who did not speak Portuguese.

Over the years, I spoke to at least eight doctors who shared how amazed they were at what they personally witnessed.

David was experiencing and seeing what I had been sharing and began to understand. I encouraged him to get the massage

David and Diane at the Casa in Brazil

which, after he did, he described as a feeling of leaving his body and seeing a mystical white light. It was so phenomenal that he set a massage appointment for our subsequent trip to be sure he got one.

Little did I know at the time, that I'd be taking people to Brazil for the next 11 years, until 2013, when I decided it was time to retire. I never charged a penny for what I did. In fact, David and I often sponsored people if they couldn't afford the cost of the trip. It warmed my heart knowing what was waiting for the people. Besides, I got to hear all those miraculous healing stories.

* * *

Ordained in "Celebrating Life Ministry," with Ron Roth, 1997

2004: After experiencing João, and all the other spiritual things that seemed to be happening, I decided to become an ordained minister in Ron's Celebrating Life Ministry Church.

It was almost like going to counseling again, only this time I had questions to answer that caused me to think and respond in writing. It was hard steady work reading book after book, listening to tapes, doing community work, and forming and presiding over a meditation group. I became an ordained minister in November, 2006.

Who would have thought I'd come this far after the life I had lived early on when, as a little girl, I was asking *Who was God? What was God?* I had always loved hearing about God or Jesus and the angel stories and pictures. It was, and is, all about the meaning of love and caring of self, as well as others—all of creation.

Two different couples asked me to preside over their marriages in Native American Indian style. As a result, I was learning again, and loving it as always. I also performed the wedding for my daughter Wendy and her new hubby. How many mothers get to do that? Fun.

* * *

During years in Madison, I took my teaching and ministry skills on the road, so to speak, doing work that matched my lifelong passions and interests.

I was involved with ARC Community Services Drug and Alcohol Program for women and their children. Some of the women and families had been homeless. Some in jail or dealing with prostitution and mental health issues. Current research suggests that practicing spirituality is one of the most critical components of recovery.

I worked with the Meriter Hospital Community Health Education Center, teaching two classes I had developed, *Happiness Comes from Within* and *Circle of Stones*, both of which focus on the potential in all of us to deepen spiritual awareness in the everyday moments of our lives.

At the East Madison Community Center, I taught a class designed for women seeking tools for finding personal fulfillment and internal resources for happiness in life, regardless of circumstances or fortune.

At Middleton Alternative Senior High School, I taught in the MASH Program, helping 17- to 18-year-old boys develop life skills.

And I was asked to be on the Lake Monona Water Walk administrative team community event to raise awareness, appreciation, and gratitude for the waters of the Madison community and the world.

* * *

Ron Roth, who had introduced me to Brazil, now told me about the Oneness University in India, as I continued on my path of learning. My daughter, Becky, and I traveled to the foothills of the Velikonda Range on the eastern coast of southern India where we stayed for a month.

Oneness University's huge pearly white structure was established in 1996, as a spiritual organization. Inner transformation and awakening are the primary goals. Soothing sounds could be heard throughout the three-story, windowless building. The setting created a peaceful learning atmosphere for people to leave behind miseries and suffering and become conscious of their individuality.

Becky and I joined others from around the world as we meditated or listened to lectures and stories of India's history and current beliefs about spirituality. We attended sacred ceremonies, danced, and did chanting that resonated within one's heart.

One day, while still in India and 7,916 miles from home, one of my teeth began to hurt. I decided to ignore it and take some pain pills I had with me. But they were not strong enough.

Here I was, another experience was about to present itself.

I went to the university office to tell them about my tooth pain. I spoke to a very kind understanding man who made an appointment with a dentist and arranged transportation for the hour-long drive.

I said, "I know your tradition does not allow for a hug, but if it did, I would give you one in appreciation." At that instant I extended my arms in a horseshoe shape to indicate a hug. We did not hug, but he commented that I was correct, but that they do hug at home. I left the office feeling good knowing the tooth would soon be taken care of.

It was early afternoon when the car and driver arrived. The kind man from the office walked past and stopped to ask how I was feeling. He wished me luck and then extended his arms in the horseshoe shape like he was giving me a virtual hug.

Wait, there's more. The dentist was kind. He looked at my tooth and we decided I would wait to have my dentist at home treat it. He gave me stronger pain pills. I was feeling relieved and said, "I know your culture doesn't allow hugs..." I started to extend my arms in the horseshoe shape when the dentist, unexpectedly, gave me the biggest hug. An actual real hug.

Then he put his arm around my shoulder and led me into his office. There were two articles on his bulletin board about the importance of hugging; the importance of human touch.

* * *

Over the years, as I was continuing to teach classes, becoming an ordained minister, working with domestic violence victims, escorting people to Brazil, and traveling to India, I was also deeply involved at Unity Church. And, through the church, I got involved in a BePeace foundation course taught by Rita Marie Johnson, who had founded the Rasur Foundation Connection in Costa Rica. In the course, Rita Marie used nonviolent communication and heart connection to learn how to "feel peace"—the ability to remain coherent under stress and "speak peace"—the ability to connect with others empathically and honestly through compassionate communication. When you feel peace and speak peace, you can BePeace, and teach peace.

About a year after meeting Rita Marie Johnson, I traveled to Costa Rica, with church members who had taken the course. She gave us a private tour of the United Nations University of Peace. Early in my life, I would never have expected to be in Costa Rica touring the United Nations University of Peace. Another unexpected adventure.

One day, I decided to take a walk by myself through a nearby rainforest. It was strangely quiet and I was walking slowly in a daze of some sort. I came to a wide ravine with a swaying suspension bridge. As I started crossing, a butterfly came toward me from the other end of the bridge. I was sure it would fly away as we neared each other. Mystically, as the butterfly came closer, I could see it wasn't as small as it had appeared at first in the distance. It was the most radiant blue color I had ever seen. It touched my shoulder, turned around, went all the way back, and disappeared. *Why did it do that?*

When I came to the end of my walk, I thought of turning around to go back into the rainforest. It was truly a walking meditation; I felt it in my inner most being. There is more to life than what meets the eye. There is the unknown world that we humans have been trying to figure out for centuries upon centuries.

* * *

And still another adventure. David and I met Andre Ferrella, an internationally acclaimed artist who creates Spirit Boxes, honoring the memory and essence of soldiers who had given their lives in Iraq and Afghanistan. The goal was to procure sites for the spirit boxes in a permanent National Memorial in Washington, D.C called "The Rise of The Fallen."

The Spirit Boxes are 9 inches wide by 14 inches high, by 3.25 inches deep and made of a white pearl-looking material. The soldiers' faces show as spirit-type images through the outer covering. When interviewed, the soldiers' parents said the boxes made them feel closer to their fallen son or daughter.

I was extremely involved in trying to move the project forward, even traveling to Washington D.C., where Andre was speaking at a VFW convention. Sadly, the interest was there but

With Michelle Obama, First Lady (2010)

not the funding. He did get "The Rise of The Fallen Spirit Boxes" on display at various art galleries and veterans museums: Charles Allis Museum, Milwaukee, Wisconsin; Elmhurst Art Museum, Elmhurst, Illinois; Digital Art Museum (DAM), Berlin, Germany; Wisconsin Veterans Museum, Madison, Wisconsin, and Fluxus Headquarters, Germany, to name a few. The exhibit touched veterans and they truly liked what they saw.

As part of our efforts, I talked with Michelle Obama about the project when she was in Milwaukee. I walked up to her knowing I didn't have much time. I immediately took her hands in mine, looked into her eyes while briefly telling her what Andre and I were attempting to do with the Spirit Boxes. There just wasn't enough time for a real discussion before having my picture taken with her. Andre also had an opportunity to meet with the First Lady, but again, not enough time. At least we tried.

For the picture I wrapped my arm tightly around Michelle Obama, The First Lady of The United States, without even thinking about it, and she in turn wrapped her arm tightly and warmly around me as we were having our picture taken. I felt a deep down to earth radiating love coming off of her.

From happy-go-lucky youngster, to my darkest of dark times in life, to holding hands, hugging and having my picture taken with the charming First Lady of the United States. If I hadn't faced my fears as time passed over the years, these would never have happened.

* * *

2017: I was learning a lot about the mental, emotional, and spiritual makeup of humans. Now came the physical surgery experience that I had never personally known before. I was told I had to have triple bypass heart surgery. How did I handle that bit of news? I had absolutely no fear. It would seem that I had considered this another happening to learn from as I continued

145

being a student in the classroom of life. I actually looked forward to it.

I had been very active physically over the years. I loved climbing trees when I was young. I liked playing sports of all kinds, running, swimming, the list goes on. As I got older, I loved playing racquet ball and tennis. I still play tennis and swim outside at the community pool during the summer and indoors during the winter.

One day, my chest had felt slightly strange. I didn't think too much of it while at the same time I figured I should have it checked. I made an appointment for after our vacation. While on vacation, we had lots of relaxing fun, which included some really vigorous tennis games. In fact, I was playing the hardest, fastest, and best games I had ever played. It was great.

At the doctor's office on Friday, I was given the news and information on what the surgery would entail, followed by, "When would you like to schedule your surgery?" I thought about it for a few seconds and replied, "Let's do it on Tuesday. Why wait?" But it is also true that I had heard over the years that people do not do good work on Mondays because of just coming off a fun or busy weekend. They are slow or tired and not quite ready for work. So, Tuesday was better.

The surgery went fine. Was there pain? You bet. My family gathered with me. The nurses and doctors were so kind, gentle and fun to be with. I had my bed made, a TV, and good food. What more could a person ask for? I sort of thought of it as a hotel with room service. I love lazing in hotel rooms anyhow. It's all in the attitude.

I healed well. The doctors attributed the successful surgery and my healthy recovery to my awareness of the food I was eating and the very all-important exercise movement of my body over the years. For my age, I was in excellent shape. I was 75 years old at the time. I'm now 81 and still going strong.

Reflections

- What leads to activism? To doing more than writing Letters to the Editor or Op-eds, but actually personally, physically being involved in a cause?

- What causes could draw you in so deeply you felt a need to help others understand your passion for the idea; your support for the cause?

CHAPTER 15

CLOSING—
MY AMAZING,
UNBELIEVABLE JOURNEY

L ooking back, after writing my life story, I see it as reminiscing, or better yet, as a movie. I always loved having my mom take my brother, Bob, and me to the movies. When I think of a movie, I can envision my life as it played out.

Hindsight is a wonderful thing in that respect. It's like looking in a rear-view mirror after you've driven past something or someone.

My movie starts with a vision of me coming into this world during a blizzard and my dad risking his life, arriving from a distance away, to be there when his new baby was about to be born.

I see me as a fun-loving little girl, full of life, running through a field of daisies with my hair blowing in the breeze. In another scene from my life movie, I'm sitting in church with my little pink elephant purse and expecting to maybe see Jesus.

Positive feelings come with those memories, which I hold on to.

Our family move to Sheboygan was already starting to teach me fear of the unknown, as I was leaving my friends behind. But as young as I was, I learned to live with it. As the years passed and we as a family continued to move from place to place, that happy little girl was fading. Here is where, watching the movie of my past, I get sad.

I can see my parents getting lost in the lives they were living, not knowing how to find answers, help or direction, and turning to the crutch of drinking alcohol, which slowly took them into more depression and misery. It was destroying them.

When I could no longer live in fear of the physical beatings I might get when Dad was in a drunken rage, I had to run, not knowing what else to do. I married at age 17 and had the first, of my four beautiful daughters, at age 18.

I was young and not knowing my own mind. There was a world out there waiting for me. But what was it?

I had been raised to do as I was told by my parents and the church, (or as the church would say, God). I became an obedient wife, doing any and everything -- way too much actually -- but I was being obedient.

As I learned of my then husband's affairs with other women, I again experienced deep pain like I had when living at home with my parents. I desperately needed help. I turned to a priest, who sent me to a psychologist, who sent me to counseling. I chose not to go the drug or alcohol route as my parents had done. At least I had learned that good lesson from them; drugs and alcohol were not the answer.

Filled with intense fear that I knew I had to face, I decided on a divorce. I didn't have a high school diploma (I had quit school to get married), no job, (we had been self-employed), no friends, (what friends we had were his), and no family support. I would be 100 percent alone raising four beautiful daughters. I found that the pain of staying in such a marriage was greater than the reward I falsely believed I had. It was like having to get out of the dark in order to see the light.

CLOSING

Being single turned out to be a blessing. I found out I was a person with feelings, wants, and desires, maybe for the first time in my life. I finished high school, went to college, and discovered I was smarter than I had been led to believe. I dared to join clubs not knowing anyone at first. I went to self-help classes. I met new friendly people of all kinds, many of them are still my friends today. I was learning that facing my fears opened doors I never thought possible.

I always liked pushing a pencil, sitting behind a desk pretending I was doing important business work as a professional. That dream came true. I walked tall wearing a suit and high heels, and got to drive a company car, which had been part of my goal too. What is interesting is that after I fulfilled that dream, I was ready for something new. A new goal.

I was learning that to be happy I had to find it within myself, someone else could not do it for me. I could not live through others.

In my movie—in my mind's eye, as I see my life during those early learning stages—I recognize how other people have had to find their way as well. I was learning that life isn't ever just for me, or just about me, or just about you. I was learning that we are all looking for the same things (like love, comfort, security, trust, and belonging) just coming from different directions and different life styles, somewhat based on our computer brain programing starting the day we are born. We really are more alike than different.

As I was learning about the human world, I was also learning about nature. When thinking of my life, in movie form, I can see me rolling in the grass or picking those beautiful flowers for my mom. I have to smile remembering playing in the rain and memories of my special animals, and even those long-legged little insects that always seem so creepy. I was learning that it was all about life and living and the fact that the human race cannot exist separately from the natural world.

Religion was re-emerging too, maybe through my connection with the mysteries of Mother Earth. I was starting to deprogram and reprogram my computer brain, not with teachings based on someone else's belief system, but my awakening to and awareness of the meaning of my own life experiences. That old programming had frightened me into believing that if I questioned the teachings of the church, I would be punished by God.

Venturing out of my safety zone, after having been afraid for far too long, I saw religion in this new light. I was on a path showing me the true way to love, caring, and happiness. I loved continuing to grow. And even with this new awakening, I continued to read book after book about Jesus. I cannot explain in human terms why I had been so attached to Jesus, even as a young child, but it continued.

David and I were married, just as that little voice had said would happen, once I started working at my new job. He and I were on the same path growing in our spiritual awareness.

Life was presenting opportunities to me as I opened to these new ways of living and thinking. On a silent weekend retreat, while sitting in chapel, a small inner voice spoke to me saying, *Quit your job, I have other things for you to do*. David agreed and within three weeks, I was out of my job, not knowing what was coming next. I seemed to have an inner knowing that I was doing the right thing.

I then traveled to India, Brazil, and Costa Rica. Why and how did I happen to be there? It hadn't been a goal of mine. But I was doing things like being on horseback high in the Himalayan mountains. I still hold mental pictures of a family living in a tent made of rags, gurus covered in white ash on bare skin, and 5000-year-old temples where I participated in traditional rituals. I saw things I had only previously seen in books.

CLOSING

Meditating en route to Brazil. Notice the daisy fly-swatter the author used to get groups through airports

John of God at the Casa, in Brazil, was beyond belief. The love I and others felt there was real. My heart was opened. Life somehow steered me into taking people there for 11 years, which I had never dreamt of doing. Helping people to witness John of God somehow tickled my insides, I was always so happy for the love and/or healing they would take home with them.

In later years, John has been convicted of sex offenses. What I see is that that is the human side of who he is. But the miracles he accomplished are on the spiritual side—the unknown. I continue to feel the love and healing.

In Costa Rica, at the United Nations of Peace, I visited my new friend, Rita Marie Johnson, who founded the BePeace program that became law in the school system there, and was later taught at the United Nations University of Peace. How did it happen that Rita Marie went to Brazil with me, stayed at my house, and became my friend?

If I had not listened to that little voice that spoke clearly to me in the silence, if I had been too afraid to quit my job, if I had played it safe, I would never have had those outstanding experiences. I cannot explain the how or why of it all, but I had learned to face my fears.

Education and learning about new things always brought more confidence. Maybe that's why I had no fear knowing I was going to have heart surgery.

As the years have played out, I developed a burning desire to help others, primarily women, but men needed to be helped too. We all suffer at some time or other, in some way or another. It's called life!

I started teaching at a college, which was something I had not expected, but I loved helping others awaken to growth. The evaluations handed in by adult students were mostly marked as *Excellent*, with positive comments. This encouraged me to go into the community helping people involved in domestic violence, or those coming out of jail or prison. I developed a passion for helping those in despair, those who are lost stumbling around in the dark trying to find their way to happiness, and those wanting to lessen their emotional as well as physical pain.

My movie, as I watch it, makes it clear that I love and have a need to help others. Life prepared me for just that.

It's time to finish my story of 81 years. My life, filled with its twists and turns and surprises around each corner, has been very full.

> *We Live, We Die,*
> *We Love Laugh Pray and Cry,*
> *What a Mysterious World This Is*

I believe nothing in the world really belongs to us/you. Snow will melt through your fingers. Vehicles, homes, clothes, money – all deteriorates, returns to dust over time and all return to nature –

David and Diane

just as the human body does. Everything is on loan – even our loved ones.

When asked what did it all mean, or even the "why" of it all, I like to reply, "Look to the sky. Where does it end? I can't comprehend it, can you?"

Yes, it's called a purpose-driven life of helping others.

Appendix

Here are comments and further information about my work roles as I took my teaching and ministry skills on the road.

2005: ARC Community Services Drug and Alcohol Day Treatment and Intensive Outpatient Program that serves women and their children.

"This can be a difficult population to work with given their many serious issues and not just anyone can join and connect with these women. It takes a 'down to earth,' authentic, and compassionate individual with a hopeful outlook that becomes contagious.

Diane is one of those individuals. She agreed to come and share her journey and to nurture the women as they learned about how to be happy and how that happiness is really a spiritual journey. Current research suggests that helping recovering addicts develop and practice spirituality is one of the most critical components of recovery.

Many of the women ARC serves have been through multiple treatment episodes and have multiple issues. Some of the women are in jail, some live in the community, while some are homeless and jobless. Many have deficits in parenting or may have prostitution issues and/or mental health issues as well as drug and alcohol issues. 100% of them have suffered many types of traumas in their lifetime.

The women loved her presentations and couldn't wait for her to arrive on Friday afternoons. Their evaluations couldn't say enough about the hope, inspiration, and love they received during their time together. They also reported that they felt that they wanted to practice walking the spiritual path they had been exploring with Diane."

2005: **Meriter Hospital Community Health Education Center** where I taught for years.

"Diane has received wonderful evaluations from her students. Two classes in particular, 'Happiness Comes from Within' and 'Circle of Stones,' focus on the potential in all of us to deepen spiritual awareness in the everyday moments of our lives.

Diane is able to capture the hearts and minds of her students, so they leave with an enriched repertoire of strategies with which to rediscover their divine essence. She enjoys being of service through teaching others with love and sincerity, and those blessed to be in her classes experience uplifted hearts."

2005: **East Madison Community Center** "The class was designed for women seeking tools for finding personal fulfillment and internal resources for happiness in life, regardless of circumstances or fortune.

The course materials were thought-provoking and targeted experiences and situations found in 'everyday life.' As a consequence, all the participants found personal ways of relating to what was being discussed. Issues of spirituality, growth and experiential learning in life were addressed weekly, as well as a wide range of individual topics like women's health, nutrition, and other factors that significantly influence how one relates to oneself, others and the world at-large.

The topic of women's spirituality was especially important to the workshop series as Diane helped participants explore what it means to understand and develop one's spiritual connections to one's self and the rest of creation. Using both simple and complex ideas and examples, participants received a much clearer understanding about how spirituality infuses all layers of existence from the mundane to the profound.

This course was very popular, as was Diane herself as a presenter."

Appendix

Middleton Alternative Senior High School —MASH Program—Life Skills

I was asked to speak to a group of 17- to 18-year-old boys who were
on a different path to graduate from high school because of disciplinary
problems.

I wasn't sure what to expect, but found the boys to be easy to talk to. I
didn't stay with ordinary topics. I spoke differently than most teachers
would. I went in deep using stories of happenings in my life as examples.

At the end of the class a number of boys came up to me asking questions. I
remember one boy in particular told me about his mom while asking what
he could do to help her.

**Interview by The Common Woman—Biannual Publication, Domestic
Abuse Intervention Services**

I was interviewed for their biannual publication. Little did I know at the
time of interview that my life story, along with my picture, was going to
be on the front page, continuing on the inside of their 12-page biannual
publication, that goes out to thousands of domestic abuse intervention services supporters. It was quite an honor.

Lake Monona Water Walk

I was asked to be on the administrative team community event to raise
awareness, appreciation, and gratitude for the waters of the Madison community and the world. The Lake Monona Water Walk and Community
Festival was a weekend full of water related inspirational and educational
events open to the public. The festival was filled with music and all kinds
of events that were both fun and educational.

One Sunday, hundreds of citizens walked the 12-mile loop around Lake
Monona. They also joined in an All-Traditions Water Blessing which was
led by two world renowned water souls, First Nations Ojibway grandmother Josephine Mandamin, and water researcher, William Waterway
Marks, author of *The Holy Order of Water and Water Voices from Around
the World.*

159

For me this meant meeting and working with the mayor, as well as other city leaders in planning and executing the community wide event. I was deeply involved and loved it reconnecting with my love of the natural world.

* * *

EARTH'S TEN COMMANDMENTS
From *Ectopia*, a novel by Ernest Callenbach (1975)

Thou Shalt Love and Honor the Earth
For It Blesses Thy Life and Governs Thy Survival;

Thou Shalt Keep Each Day Sacred to The Earth
And Celebrate the Turning Of its Seasons;

Thou Shalt Not Hold Thyself Above Other Living Things
Nor Drive Them to Extinction;

Thou Shalt Give Thanks for Thy Food and To the Creatures
And Plants That Nourish Thee;

Thou Shalt Limit Thy Offspring
For Multitudes of People Are a Burden unto The Earth;

Thou Shalt Not Kill nor Waste Earth's Riches
Upon Weapons of War;

Thou Shalt Not Pursue Profit at The Earth's Expense
But Strive to Restore its Damaged Majesty;

Thou Shat Not Hide from Thyself or Others
The Consequences of Thy Actions Upon the Earth;

Thou Shalt Not Steal from Future Generations
By Impoverishing Or Poisoning the Earth;

Thou Shalt Consume Material Goods in Moderation
So, All May Share Earths Bounty

* * *

The Golden Rule in Many of the World's Great Religions

*"Do onto others as you would have them do onto you –
for you will be doing it onto yourself."*

Baha'i: "And if thine eyes be turned toward justice, choose thou for your neighbor that which thou choosest for thyself."

Christianity: "All things whatsoever ye would that men should do to you, do ye even so to them."

Confucianism: "Do not unto others what you would not they should do unto you."

Buddhism: "In five ways should a clansman minister to his friends and familiars – by generosity, courtesy and benevolence, by treating them as he treats himself, and by being as good as his word."

Hinduism: "Do not to others, which if done to thee, would cause thee pain."

Mohammedanism: "No one of you is a believer until he loves for his brother what he loves for himself."

Sikhism: "As thou deemest thyself so deem others. Then shalt thou become a partner in heaven."

Hebraism: "What is hurtful to yourself, do not to your fellow man."

Jainism: "In happiness and suffering, in joy and grief, we should regard all creatures as we regard our own self."

Zoroastrianism: "That nature only is good when it shall not do unto another whatsoever is not good for its own self."

Taoism: "Regard your neighbor's gain as your own gain and regard your neighbor's loss as your own loss."

AN AMAZING (26)
ACKNOWLEDGMENTS

All I can say is, "Thank You."

This isn't just about writing a book, it's about a lifetime of sharing the mysterious workings of the world. I have been on a path in life, and what an amazing life it has been. Each and every one of you has been there with me somehow, somewhere, at some time or other. I could not have grown forward without you as you and I were becoming teachers and students in the classroom of life. It's not possible to name each of you beautiful souls, but a few key players include:

Thank you, Mom and Dad. You taught the basics of life and living through negative as well as positive experiences while I lived with you. Times weren't always easy, but I'm happy with who I am today, that's the important thing. Dad, what I loved about you most was the gentle soul you were, because it taught me what gentle feels like. And Mom, what I loved about you the most was the fun in your soul, full of music, dancing and laughter. I love you both, even though you passed on many years ago.

Brother Bob. I love and miss you. Even though you are no longer with us today I will always cherish the time we had together, while remembering you as such a character, always making me laugh.

Cousin LaVonne, what can I say? I am ever so grateful for your taking me in that dark scary night I ran away from home. You were always like a sister to me. When thinking of you I think of those crazy things we used to do as kids like pretending we were talking a foreign language—and I mean pretending. Remember the giggling? Fun, fun, fun!

As a little girl, Jesus' messages taught me what my soul longed to hear—it's all about love—loving others as self. I wasn't always able to think in terms of love during painful, hard times, but life itself, along with Jesus' messages, taught me the importance of love in all that we do in order to produce and live in happiness.

During a very dark time in my life, I found counseling to be one of many ways that helped lead me out of the dark and into the light. I went to counseling for over two years where I joined a circle of women, each of us sharing stories of how we lost our way. How do I say thank you to a beautiful group of women who helped me to open my eyes to the fact that most of us humans are more alike than different, that I'm not an oddball out after all, as life had led me to believe.

I loved walking and sometimes roller-skating outside with a group of women. We called ourselves "The Walkie Talkies." In other words, we walked as much as we talked. Having such wonderful women to share life with was priceless. Thank you, Walkie Talkies, for the fun-filled times we had together.

Many thanks go out to the schools, colleges, churches, teachers, professors, self-growth programs, social clubs, the list goes on. So many people from these organizations entered my life when I needed them most. Little did I know what I was learning as I was growing forward with them.

Thank you to those I met during my travels to Brazil, India, and Costa Rica who all added to my lessons in life as I met and learned about their life styles and beliefs. They taught me so much about another part of the world. I found them to be loving, kind people who made me feel right at home. We were more alike than different.

ACKNOWLEDGMENTS

Nature, Mother Earth, and all its creatures—how can I say thank you enough for your abundance (without it we would perish) given to us in all its beauty and wonder by that mystery creator, be it God, the Divine, the Higher Power, the Universe, or what or whomever you choose.

I have to thank my first husband, Phillip, who was there for me when my life, living with my parents, was torn apart. He and I were oh so young; little did we know what the future had in store for us with its twists and turns!

To Pam, Wendy, Dawn, and Becky, my four beautiful daughters, I say thank you for staying at my side through painful as well as fun-loving times. For this reason, I sometimes like to say we grew up together. I cannot express enough the love I have for you.

I am so blessed to have had six grandsons, Eric, Johnathon, Alex, Kyle, Anthony, and Austin, and three granddaughters, Amanda, Amber, and Olivia. And I can't forget my four precious little great-grandchildren, Coraley, Zayden, Isabella, and Eric. It's fun watching all of you grow forward as life presents itself. I'm hoping you will read my story and learn some of the ways to head off pain. Sending a loving thank-you for being you.

David, a loving and caring husband, you have been on a path in life with me. You have been so supportive as I ventured out into the world seeking to find what life was all about. You were there as I was always seeking answers to the why of it all, even when a silent little voice within me said, "Quit your job, I have other things for you to do." Little did you or I know the whirlwind of life that was waiting for us. I have truly been blessed having you at my side. "I love you, my honey."

An added note, I have to say thank you to that little voice within me, that inner knowing voice, that was always there to guide me on the path "Called Life." Wow, what a mysterious, unbelievable journey you took me on!

A Purpose-Driven Life

* * * *

Thank you to Harvey Honig for writing the Foreword to this book. Harvey, I know you to be a gentle soul with love in your heart. I feel honored having you take the time to express your thoughts on the message contained in my unbelievable life story.

To you beautiful souls—Peg Hau, Marianne Helm, Pamela Hertel, and Paul Funfsinn—who took time out of your busy lives to read my story, I can only say thank you. Your comments made me feel humble in the ways you describe me and the message in my life story.

Amber DeAmico, with a talented eye for beautiful photography, thank you so much for walking through the fields with me until we found my daisy field for the cover of my book. (Did I mention Amber is my gifted granddaughter and Amanda's sister?)

Amanda DeAmico, so quick with creative design mastering attractive business cards, a talented young lady to say the least. Thank you so much for being there for me. (Did I mention that Amanda is my gifted granddaughter and Amber's sister?)

And I would like to thank my co-author, Judith Gwinn Adrian, who wasn't just an editor, but also my teacher with the patience of an angel. Judith saw more than just an autobiography in me; she also saw my story as a way for giving a guiding hand to those searching for answers to the "Why" of it all.

And a thank you to my publisher, Kira Henschel, of HenschelHAUS Publishing, Inc. for also seeing a story that needed to be shared. She sensed a burning desire in me, like I was on a purposed-filled mission in life to help others—she is right.

ABOUT THE AUTHORS

Because of an abusive history, Diane Pauly has spent most of her life developing a deeper understanding of personal happiness and well-being. She returned to finish high school at the age of 35, then earned her associate degree in materials management and bachelor of arts degree in business administration and psychology. Diane also studied to become an ordained minister. She attended numerous self-growth programs/classes locally as well as around the world, including lectures, intensives, workshops, and retreats given by well-known educators. Diane has taught spiritually-infused healing classes and lectured at such places as the UW–Sheboygan; Mental Health Services; Wholistic Health Center; Meriter Hospital, Madison; ARC Community Services, Madison, and Sojourner Family Peace Center, Milwaukee, to name a few. She has worked with people involved with domestic violence and those who had been incarcerated in jails and prisons.

Diane currently lives in Plymouth, Wisconsin, with her loving husband David, and their two precious little doggies, Missy and Chloe.

Website: www.dianepauly.com

Judith Gwinn Adrian, co-author

Diane and Judith became a team, organizing and writing this memoir, mostly via Zoom meetings during the Covid-19 pandemic. An adventure. After retiring from 25 years of teaching at Edgewood College in Madison, WI, Adrian has written and/or co-written ten books. Each of the books has been its own journey of storytelling.

There is more detailed information at judithadrian.com.